# Managing Human Resources in Small and Medium-sized Enterprises

Well-managed employment relationships can be a secret to business success, yet this factor is relatively poorly understood when it comes to small and medium-sized enterprises (SMEs).

Written by active researchers with teaching experience, this book brings together the fields of entrepreneurship and human resource management (HRM) for the first time, providing entrepreneurship students with a solid grounding in HRM as well as a platform for further critical engagement with the research. The concise and authoritative style also enables the book to be used as a primer for researchers exploring this under-developed terrain.

As the only student-focused specialist book on human resource management in entrepreneurial firms, this is vital reading for students and researchers in this area, as well as those interested in small business and management more generally.

**Robert Wapshott** is Senior Lecturer in Entrepreneurship at the University of Sheffield, UK.

**Oliver Mallett** is Lecturer in Management at Durham University, UK.

# Routledge Masters in Entrepreneurship

Edited by Janine Swail

The **Routledge Masters in Entrepreneurship** series offers postgraduate students specialist but accessible textbooks on a range of entrepreneurship topics. Collectively, these texts form a significant resource base for those studying entrepreneurship, whether as part of an entrepreneurship-related programme of study, or as a new, non-cognate area for students in disciplines such as science and engineering, helping them to gain an in-depth understanding of contemporary entrepreneurial concepts.

The volumes in this series are authored by leading specialists in their field, and although they are discrete texts in their treatment of individual topics, all are united by a common structure and pedagogical approach. Key features of each volume include:

- A critical approach to combining theory with practice, which educates its reader rather than solely teaching a set of skills
- Clear learning objectives for each chapter
- The use of figures, tables and boxes to highlight key ideas, concepts and skills
- An annotated bibliography, guiding students in their further reading, and
- Discussion questions for each chapter to aid learning and put key concepts into practice.

**Entrepreneurship**
A global perspective
*Stephen Roper*

**Female Entrepreneurship**
*Maura McAdam*

**Resourcing the Start-Up Business**
Creating dynamic entrepreneurial learning capabilities
*Oswald Jones, Allan Macpherson and Dilani Jayawarna*

**Entrepreneurship, Small Business and Public Policy**
Evolution and revolution
*Robert J. Bennett*

**Finance for Small and Entrepreneurial Businesses**
*Richard Roberts*

**Managing Human Resources in Small and Medium-Sized Enterprises**
Entrepreneurship and the employment relationship
*Robert Wapshott and Oliver Mallett*

# Managing Human Resources in Small and Medium-sized Enterprises

Entrepreneurship and the employment relationship

Robert Wapshott and Oliver Mallett

LONDON AND NEW YORK

First published 2016
by Routledge
2 Park Square, Milton Park, Abingdon, Oxon OX14 4RN

and by Routledge
711 Third Avenue, New York, NY 10017

*Routledge is an imprint of the Taylor & Francis Group, an informa business*

© 2016 Robert Wapshott and Oliver Mallett

The right of Robert Wapshott and Oliver Mallett to be identified as authors of this work has been asserted by them in accordance with sections 77 and 78 of the Copyright, Designs and Patents Act 1988.

All rights reserved. No part of this book may be reprinted or reproduced or utilised in any form or by any electronic, mechanical, or other means, now known or hereafter invented, including photocopying and recording, or in any information storage or retrieval system, without permission in writing from the publishers.

*Trademark notice*: Product or corporate names may be trademarks or registered trademarks, and are used only for identification and explanation without intent to infringe.

*British Library Cataloguing in Publication Data*
A catalogue record for this book is available from the British Library

*Library of Congress Cataloging in Publication Data*
Wapshott, Robert.
 Managing human resources in small and medium-sized enterprises: entrepreneurship and the employment relationship/Robert Wapshott and Oliver Mallett.
  pages cm. -- (Routledge ISBE masters in entrepreneurship)
Includes bibliographical references and index.
 1. Small business--Employees. 2. Small business--Personnel management. I. Mallett, Oliver. II. Title.
 HD2341.W337 2016
 658.3--dc23
              2015012650

ISBN: 978-1-138-80518-7 (hbk)
ISBN: 978-1-138-80519-4 (pbk)
ISBN: 978-1-315-75247-1 (ebk)

Typeset in Bembo
by Taylor & Francis Books
Printed by Ashford Colour Press Ltd.

# Contents

*List of illustrations* vi

**PART I**
**The distinctive case of SMEs**    **1**

1 Introduction    3

2 From entrepreneur to owner-manager    19

3 Shaping employment relationships in SMEs    31

**PART II**
**Managing human resources**    **47**

4 Recruitment and selection    49

5 Training and development    63

6 Reward and recognition    78

7 Staff turnover    95

**PART III**
**Rethinking HRM in SMEs**    **109**

8 SME growth, HRM and the role of formalisation    111

9 Employment relationships and practices in SMEs    124

10 Conclusion: the management of human resources in SMEs    137

*Bibliography*    148
*Index*    161

# List of illustrations

## Tables

| | |
|---|---:|
| 1.1 Estimated number of businesses in the UK private sector and their associated employment and turnover, by size of business, start of 2014 | 4 |
| 3.1 Influences on employment relationships and practices | 44 |
| 4.1 Sources of potential employees | 50 |
| 5.1 Influences on training in SMEs | 67 |

## Boxes

| | |
|---|---:|
| Task 1.1 | 9 |
| Task 1.2 | 11 |
| Task 2.1 | 20 |
| Task 2.2 | 25 |
| Task 3.1 | 37 |
| Task 3.2 | 39 |
| Task 4.1 | 49 |
| Task 4.2 | 54 |
| Task 4.3 | 60 |
| Task 5.1 | 68 |
| Task 6.1 | 82 |
| Task 6.2 | 86 |
| Task 6.3 | 93 |
| Task 8.1 | 122 |

# Part I
# The distinctive case of SMEs

# 1 Introduction

Small and medium-sized enterprises (SMEs) employ significant numbers of people in the world's major economies. For example, in the UK broad definitions of SMEs account for over 5 million businesses and the paid employment of 15 million people (see Table 1.1). With so many people either self-employed or employed in SMEs, the quality of their employment relationships has implications for a great many working lives. Moreover, for those wanting to manage their own small or medium-sized business successfully, and for governments wanting to develop policies that will help and not hinder these firms, we need to explore the relationships and practices found within them.

In different guises SMEs have been around as long as businesses have, although not always in fashion and often ignored. In modern economies focused on economic growth, SMEs have been given a central place in the narratives offered up by politicians and lobby groups as a way to solve economic malaise, provide economies with a transfusion of energy, innovation and disruption, while providing economic growth and employment. Cast in their current heroic guise, it becomes easy to overlook the messiness that characterises aspects of SMEs on a day-to-day basis as they seek to cope with various challenges. In this book we are interested in moving beyond the political rhetoric and somewhat simplistic characterisations of SMEs to try to understand the complexities and messiness of everyday employment relationships and practices.

One of the most prominent measures of success for SMEs is business growth in terms of employment expansion. Yet how employees are recruited, selected and managed in these firms remains under-explored and mainstream textbooks on both human resource management (HRM) and entrepreneurship pay little, if any, attention to understanding employment relationships in SMEs. This oversight matters because ignoring or misunderstanding the issues associated with the employment relationship could hold back start-up ventures and present barriers to enterprise success. Creating and running a successful enterprise relies on more than just the start-up phase; it is vital not to overlook the management of businesses and the role of employees.

In this book we present a discussion of people management (or 'human resource management' as it is commonly known) in small and medium-sized enterprises, with a particular focus on entrepreneurial firms, which we define very broadly as those that are experiencing growth or are taking steps to fulfil their aspirations for business growth. We draw on a wide range of literature to offer interesting perspectives on important aspects of human resource management in SMEs, arguing that they are often distinct from larger firms and need to be understood on their own terms. Our approach will provide students with a foundation of core knowledge around employment issues in these organisations and also a platform for further critical engagement with debates in the research. For lecturers this text will offer flexibility in how they tailor their classes to student knowledge and ability. Students who will benefit most from grasping the core information and concepts can be focused on the substantive topics covered in the book, while those with a sound grasp of these topics can be challenged through the more critical and analytical themes underpinning the text. This structure will also enable the book to be used as a primer for student dissertations and for researchers who are interested in engaging with this area of study.

In this first chapter we will outline our perspective on employment relationships and practices in SMEs, introduce ourselves as authors and provide an overview of the book's structure.

## SMEs, employment and the economy

In many economies around the world, SMEs constitute the majority of business enterprises. Look at the UK, USA and, with changes in recent years, former communist states such as Estonia and you will find that SMEs represent somewhere over 90% of all private business enterprises and account for significant proportions of non-governmental employment. If we return to the example of the UK (see Table 1.1), we can see just how significant a role SMEs play in terms of business enterprises and employment. Discounting the self-employed,

*Table 1.1* Estimated number of businesses in the UK private sector and their associated employment and turnover, by size of business, start of 2014

|  | Businesses | Employment (thousands) | Turnover (£ millions) |
| --- | --- | --- | --- |
| All businesses | 5,243,135 | 25,229 | 3,521,254 |
| SMEs (0–249 employees) | 5,236,390 | 15,159 | 1,647,201 |
| Small businesses (0–49 employees) | 5,204,915 | 12,084 | 1,170,337 |
| All employers | 1,277,360 | 20,876 | 3,290,110 |
| With no employees | 3,965,775 | 4,353 | 231,143 |
| 1–9 employees (micro) | 1,044,385 | 3,923 | 424,299 |
| 10–49 employees (small) | 194,755 | 3,807 | 514,895 |
| 50–249 (medium) | 31,475 | 3,075 | 476,864 |
| 250 or more (large) | 6,745 | 10,070 | 1,874,053 |

Source: Adapted BIS, 2014.

SMEs provide around 10 million jobs within the UK economy, or over 40% of the non-government jobs total presented by the Office for National Statistics. SMEs are also acknowledged to *create* jobs, although we must remember that many SMEs fail and so they also account for a high proportion of job losses (see Anyadike-Danes *et al.*, 2011). It is also important to note that many SMEs have no employees beyond the lone business owner or group of partners who own the venture (see Table 1.1).

The number of businesses and employees means that, in the UK alone, studying the employment relationships and practices in SMEs can tell us important things about the working experiences of millions of people. Readers from outside the UK may wish to take a moment to look up the role played by SMEs within the economy in their home country. While there are differences in terminology and definition that mean we must be careful when drawing international comparisons, the general picture is one where, although many businesses are quite small, the sheer number of them means that SMEs can account for high numbers of jobs. Clearly, understanding the employment relationships and practices within these kinds of businesses is an important element in understanding work in modern societies.

This means that many of the people reading this book will, at some point in their working lives, have business relations with SMEs, whether that be as an owner, an employee, a supplier or a client. If you run your own business currently, then the contents of our book might chime with your experiences to date, and in doing so serve to counter-balance some of the more prescriptive models of people management that seem to treat a large firm experience as typical while paying scant attention to SMEs more generally. We are less interested in prescribing apparently 'best practice' than we are in understanding how employment relationships and practices develop in SMEs, taking these businesses, and the practices that are in use within them, on their own terms.

This understanding will not come from the application of knowledge gained from multinational corporations. As this book will show, employment relationships can differ significantly in SMEs compared with what you might have studied in more general courses on HRM which have a tendency to emphasise the challenges and responses of much larger organisations (Baron, 2003). Consequently, if our knowledge only comes from large firms, or we otherwise fail to understand SMEs on their own terms, we can have a distorted understanding of the employment relationships and practices that represent the everyday working lives of millions of people.

## Why SMEs matter to us

For all the quantifiable reasons why we think employment relationships in SMEs are interesting, there are also more personal reasons for our interest in the topic. At the time of writing, Robert has studied employment in small firms for around ten years. His interest in the topic area stems from his MBA studies, when he began to wonder why the various models of HRM he was studying seemed to say little or nothing about working lives in small firms. He pursued this interest through his PhD, during which he studied the employment relationships of small firms in detail. Currently he teaches the module 'Entrepreneurship and Human Resource Management' at the University of Sheffield, where he forms part of the Centre for Regional Economic and Enterprise Development. He is also a director and trustee of the Institute for Small Business and Entrepreneurship.

Oliver has a different academic background, initially studying psychology and then exploring psychoanalytic approaches to understanding cities in his PhD. However, it was while conducting his PhD studies, when Oliver was working part time in the public sector, that he would discuss working life with his wife (Becky) who was a company director in a small IT firm. The differences in working practices and the day-to-day experiences of these contrasting jobs were striking. For example, while Oliver never interacted with those at the top of his organisation (a government department), in Becky's company all employees had formal and informal contact with the owner-manager on a regular basis. Further, where the large public-sector organisation would work on long-term strategic changes that were slow to implement, change in the IT firm was rapid and, at times, ad hoc.

After we had both completed our PhD studies, this overlap of interests led to us working on understanding home-based businesses and home working more generally in terms of social space (Wapshott and Mallett, 2012). We have since worked with a broad range of SMEs and entrepreneurs, developing our understanding and our appreciation of the complexities of employment relationships in these businesses. We have published our work in a range of academic journal articles but also in national newspapers, practitioner forums, and in company and government reports. It is upon this work, conducted over the past decade or so, that we draw in this book.

We believe strongly that the employment relationships and practices in SMEs represent a vital and fascinating topic. However, it is not a straightforward one and, before outlining the contents of the book, it is valuable to define some of our key terms.

## Getting to grips with some key terms

Before we go much further and get into a more detailed consideration of entrepreneurship and HRM it is appropriate for us to clarify our definitions. As the book progresses you will be able to develop your understanding of these areas and build some detail around these basic definitions but, for now, we will set out briefly how we use certain common words and phrases.

### *What is an entrepreneur?*

The terms 'entrepreneurship' and 'entrepreneur' have, in recent years, become widely adopted in everyday use and in the academic literature (Greene *et al.*,

2008). The terms have been subject to different uses and critical consideration (Mills, 1951; Bendix, 1956; DuGay, 1996; Jones and Spicer, 2009; Mallett and Wapshott, 2015). In this book we use the term 'entrepreneurship' to refer to the process of business foundation and 'entrepreneurs' to identify the people most closely associated with that start-up. We acknowledge that these uses are more colloquial than technically rigorous. However, they suffice as a shorthand to indicate when we are discussing the early stages of organisation foundation and when a founder may be initially setting out on their own (Greene et al., 2008).

We use the term 'owner-manager' frequently in the book. By owner-manager we mean the person who owns the business and remains closely associated with overseeing its day-to-day operation. Owner-managers are attributed a key role in SMEs where, owing to the size of the organisation, an owner can readily exercise their influence (see Goss, 1991). We take the term to imply the presence of employees in the organisation beyond the founder or founding team. From some perspectives the owner-manager may be seen as a very powerful figure in deciding how things are done in a firm and how employment issues are addressed, but, as our discussion throughout the book will show, this is not necessarily the case.

## *What is an SME?*

Small and medium-sized enterprises are defined variously in different parts of the world and in different academic texts. Number of employees has consistently been the most dominant basis for classing a firm as an SME, but alternatives incorporate annual turnover, a local focus and industry norms. Given this book's focus on the employment relationships and practices in SMEs, we will draw on these definitions and mainly focus on number of employees. As you will see as we progress through the book, defining a group of businesses on the basis of employee numbers can be problematic if it means that other important considerations such as sectoral norms are disregarded (Arrowsmith et al., 2003). While business size is a useful tool for giving an initial focus for our attention, we must always try to understand businesses in their wider context; the challenges and responses one might encounter in a small business from one industry, for instance, could differ markedly from those found in another industry.

As you conduct your own wider study of the research literature in this area, it is important to bear in mind the relevance of similarities and differences between firms and retain a questioning attitude to understand how far research based on a given set of firms can help explain the employment practices and relationships of a quite different set of firms. Where possible we will therefore identify the correct usage in terms of small, medium and so on. However, literature in this area rarely treats small and medium-sized businesses as distinct under the SME banner. Acknowledging this challenge, we present the literature as we find it, adopting the terminology used in published works. We recognise this potential limitation but will not focus unduly on this aspect of any studies we discuss, preferring to highlight the most relevant issues for the topic under discussion.

## What is human resource management?

HRM can be broadly understood as 'the management of people at work' (Bratton and Gold, 1999: 4), particularly with a view to engendering employee commitment in order to achieve superior performance outcomes for an organisation. Typically aligned with managers' perspective on the employment relationship, HRM's reference to employees as human resources can be a little off-putting but it has become the dominant terminology for a certain area of management activities, including recruitment and selection, training and development, reward and recognition and staff exit, that are conducted with a focus on achieving an organisation's goals. It is therefore a term we use in this book alongside employment relationships and practices.

Writing in 2005, Scott Taylor argues that contemporary understandings of managing employment relationships are dominated by a particular ideological approach of 'human resource management' that emphasises the application of codified professional techniques to address management problems. Management practices are derived from formal policies that are aligned with an organisation's strategy and with a degree of standardisation across the organisation. Taylor identifies that this perspective on managing issues associated with employment relationships becomes especially problematic when applied to the practices found in small businesses. Taylor demonstrates how applying HRM-informed understandings of employment relationships and practices to make sense of the workings of small firms leads to misunderstanding and limited insight. Looking for HRM in small firms risks seeking something (formally framed policies and practices) that does not really exist within the operating contexts of many small firms, while overlooking more relevant influences on their employment relationships and practices.

The approach we will adopt is to focus on the particular activities, such as staff recruitment, that are subsumed under this heading. As we work through the chapters in this book we will develop this idea of how numerous influences arising internally and externally to the firm interact to shape employment relationships and practices. We will also (see Chapter 4) consider in greater detail another of Taylor's concerns around how the application of 'HRM' to small firms results in these organisations being seen as lacking and deficient for not measuring up to the supposed ideal of HRM.

## What is the employment relationship?

Continuing in the spirit of Taylor (2005), we are interested primarily in understanding the employment relationships and practices encountered in

SMEs. We draw our focus on employment relationships from Edwards's (1995: 47–48) paper 'From industrial relations to the employment relationship', in which he locates the field of employment relations within a particularly British context and identifies:

> a focus on the organization and control of the employment relationship: the processes through which employers and employees – who are tied together in relations of mutual dependence underlain by exploitation – negotiate the performance of work tasks, together with the laws, rules, agreements and customs that shape these processes ... [this] approach is distinctive in its focus on the nature of rules governing employment, the negotiation of order, and the structural context of the relation between employer and employee within which this negotiation takes place.

When we use a term such as 'employment relationships and practices' we are referring to what is going on inside a firm between an owner-manager and employees, and the attempts of owner-managers to control parts of a relationship. We demonstrate how employment relationships and the practices in use are negotiated by actors, who are by degrees mutually dependent, in response to influences arising both outside and inside the firm. We argue that these relationships and associated practices must be understood as embedded in their wider context – for example, considerations including the firm's competitive position, its relations with clients and the state of the labour market more generally (for further discussion see Edwards, 1995; Harney and Dundon, 2006; Gilman and Edwards, 2008). From this broad focus, adopted to try to avoid an overly prescriptive sense of what is and what is not relevant in shaping employment issues in SMEs, we will highlight more specific concerns as they are discussed in the literature and research evidence.

### Task 1.1

To get started thinking about employment relationships and practices in SMEs, it is worth seeing how much you know already. Working either on your own or in a small group, sketch out a table with three columns. Think of a particular SME you know (or imagine one in a particular industry) and in the first column of your table write down as many *influences*, external and internal, that might have implications for how that business operates. For each influence, in the second column say *how* you think it might impact on the firm, and in the third column *what that might mean* for employment relationships and practices in your chosen SME.

For a very basic example: thinking of a small, fancy restaurant you might identify 'economic slowdown' in column one, 'reduced financial turnover' in column two, and 'pressure on affording staff wages' in column three.

## Do SMEs really deserve special attention when studying human resource management and employment relationships?

In aspects of entrepreneurship and small businesses, such as government policy, there is only a limited case for treating certain firms as special cases, as explained by Robert Bennett (2014) in his book *Entrepreneurship, Small Business and Public Policy* (also in this *Routledge Masters in Entrepreneurship* series). There is a case to be made that gathering organisations of similar size under a single category is an unhelpfully vague categorisation of highly heterogeneous organisations that share little in common beyond the length of their staff lists (Torrès, 2003; Cardon and Stevens, 2004). Further, as Bennett (2014) makes clear, the label can be distorted in line with political aims and interests.

It is therefore unsurprising that there have been extended debates as to whether SMEs can be considered a distinct area of management research (Torrès, 2003). This debate was played out in the pages of the *International Small Business Journal* where Torrès and Julien (2005: 355) argued against what they call 'small business managerial specificity'. Their argument was that research into smaller firms had become dominated by a stubborn assertion that small firms, predominantly defined by employee numbers, are a distinct group of organisations and are worthy of research attention on these terms. They argue (ibid.: 358) that the problem with this 'small business specificity' model is that firms employing similar numbers of employees can vary significantly in terms of other, important characteristics.

We can understand this point through a stylised example comparing a hand car-washing business and a law firm. We could identify that despite both businesses employing an equal number of people, their respective needs for employees might differ. The car-wash business can recruit new staff to perform the principal tasks for the business relatively easily, provided basic requirements are met. The law firm, on the other hand, might require only suitably qualified solicitors, who have undertaken around seven years of training, to conduct legal work. Once employed, solicitors will need to keep up to date with the law and satisfy the Solicitors Regulation Authority's requirements around continuous professional development, whereas the capabilities for working at the car wash are not regulated in a similar way. By applying a crude quantitative definition to group firms of a similar size and treating this as a cohesive grouping, 'authors are inclined to treat as certainties elements that are no more than probabilities' (Torrès and Julien, 2005: 359). That is, researchers risk over-generalising characteristics of businesses employing similar numbers of people and, in turn, risk misrepresenting what is actually happening within these firms. While it may be difficult to apply knowledge from large firms to small firms, it also seems difficult to apply knowledge gained from the car wash to understand HRM practices in the law firm.

Torrès and Julien's (2005: 360) alternative is one in which the 'specificity thesis' is subject to testing and that, in some cases, small firms may not represent a distinct grouping. They argue in favour of a contingency approach that centres on 'admitting that the validity of the specificity thesis is subject to certain conditions, and that, outside its field of application the thesis is irrelevant or obsolete' (ibid.: 360). In short, Torrès and Julien argue that their contingency approach requires researchers to account for more than just employee numbers in defining their research scope and empirical focus on firms.

The article drew a response from a longstanding and highly respected contributor to research on small businesses, James Curran (2006). In a short but detailed critique, Curran argues that Torrès and Julien's position overlooks the historical development of research into small businesses. He argues that the problems associated with defining firms simply by employee numbers are already acknowledged and addressed within the literature. Further, there has been some significant, detailed, qualitative research into these firms (much of which we will discuss in detail in this book) which has developed our understanding of these businesses, putting assumptions and generalisations to the test. Curran therefore argues that the grouping of businesses that are of similar size through the identification of similarities is rooted in years of research, rather than academic dogma as Torrès and Julien imply.

The exchange between the authors is interesting and well worth a read to help you think critically about how firms are defined and studied. Given the heterogeneity of firms under consideration, the loose grouping implied whenever we talk about SMEs will always be problematic and its limitations must be borne in mind alongside the long tradition of research into exploring the practices within these businesses. It is important to appreciate the heterogeneity of small firms as well as what they have in common.

### Task 1.2

Think about the area in which you live, study or work, and identify five small businesses.

With colleagues who have done likewise, think about how those businesses can be compared and contrasted in a general sense. For example: What products/services are they offering? Who are their clients/customers? Who might work there? What skills or qualifications might employees need? Then try to group the businesses together around some elements of commonality. What types of business can belong in one group as opposed to another group? How do the groups differ? How are the groups the same? Are there any types of business missing from the list that may differ in significant ways?

While we accept the cautionary tone of Torrès and Julien's argument, we believe it overstates their case. It is important to recognise that just because businesses large or small employ similar numbers of people, this does not make them automatically comparable on the basis of some supposed shared interests or characteristics. Al Rainnie (1991: 182) eloquently expressed this observation, warning against analysis in which 'the heterogeneity of the small firm is subsumed into a monocausal explanation of shared industrial relations characteristics'. It is not a new observation and does not seem as prevalent a problem in the employment relations literature as Torrès and Julien's position might imply. An interesting feature of research in this area is, in fact, the way that considerations of context inform analysis and discussion of employment relationships and practices as we find, for example, presented in papers by Brian Harney and Tony Dundon (2006) and Mark Gilman and Paul Edwards (2008) that we discuss later in the book.

At the same time, however, there are characteristics that might be readily associated with SMEs, such that some common ground can be identified in how these organisations operate and the types of management challenges they face. Consequently, in this book we are *not* going to argue that simply because businesses are of a certain similar size, we can lump them all together and draw broad conclusions about how their employment issues are encountered and addressed. Rather, we are interested in how characteristics associated with *many but not all* SMEs have a bearing on their employment practices and relationships. We will develop these points over the coming chapters but, for now, we can identify certain characteristics often associated with SMEs and which may suggest some of the ways in which their management of employees could differ from larger firms.

## *High degrees of informality*

Small and medium-sized enterprises are generally acknowledged to operate along more informal lines than larger businesses. Informality can exist in various ways when it comes to employment relationships and practices. It can be taken to signal an absence or limited use of written policies and practices (Marlow et al., 2010), an ad hoc way of organising and distributing tasks rather than employees having clearly defined job roles, with implications for the ways in which employment relationships are conducted on a day-to-day basis (Ram, 1994; Wapshott and Mallett, 2013).

Working along largely informal lines can allow businesses flexibility in their operations, enabling them to respond to challenges and opportunities that may present themselves. It may also reflect preferences of those owner-managers who enjoy the apparent scope it gives them to exercise their prerogative (Marlow, 2003). At the same time, however, it is not suitable for all businesses or situations and, as firms grow, there is a tendency to replace informal arrangements with more formalised ways of operating (Kotey and Sheridan, 2004) but getting optimal degrees of formality and informality is difficult (Mallett and Wapshott, 2014). We will return to discuss the issues of informality in greater detail later in the book as it is an important area of understanding employment relationships and practices in business organisations of various sizes (Ram et al., 2001).

## Spatial and social proximity

Informal ways of working distinct from those found in larger firms may emerge, in small businesses especially, from the close spatial and social proximity in which owner-managers and employees find themselves working. *Spatial proximity* refers to where owner-managers and employees may share working space, for example simply because of the small numbers of people working within the firm or perhaps owing to a focus on keeping office-rental expenditure to a minimum or through practical necessity for managing the tasks being undertaken. Owner-managers and employees working alongside each other can create degrees of *social proximity*, or closeness, through the scope for overlap between personal and working relationships (Ram, 1999) and a greater degree of familiarity in the workplace (Goss, 1991).

This spatial and social proximity can contribute to greater employee satisfaction (Tsai et al., 2007). However, it does not automatically follow that spatial and social proximity will lead to generally informal and/or positive interactions among co-workers. Close physical proximity might permit opportunities for constant close supervision of employees, which some employees might find stressful. Moreover, with their own actions on show to the rest of the business, owner-managers might find themselves open to charges of hypocrisy or, perhaps worse, incompetence as their own efforts and errors are displayed (Mallett and Wapshott, 2014). While acknowledging the potential advantages of close spatial and social proximity, we must therefore also bear in mind that these relationships retain the potential for conflicts that can be particularly disruptive (Goss, 1991; Marlow, 2003).

Nor should we conflate proximity with degrees of informality. Ram and colleagues, writing on 'The dynamics of informality: employment relations in small firms and the effects of regulatory change', argue that '[t]oo often it [informality] is accepted as an inevitable product of entrepreneurialism and close interpersonal relations in the workplace, promoting individualised and *ad hoc* patterns of decision-making and behaviour' (Ram et al., 2001: 859). Instead, the authors identify how informality is dynamic and influenced by a range of factors including trading conditions facing a business, the availability of staff and the nature of the tasks being undertaken in the business. In other words, we cannot simply conflate spatial and social proximity with relatively high degrees of informality; they might co-exist but this is not necessarily the case in all instances.

## Resource poverty

Stemming from the view that SMEs lack the resources of large organisations, 'resource poverty' describes challenges particularly facing SMEs and has been a regular theme of how these organisations are understood (Welsh and White, 1981: 18; Cassell et al., 2002). For example, Welsh and White (1981) argued that smaller firms tend to be concentrated in industries subject to price cutting, that the relative burden of owner-managers' salaries on revenues is greater in smaller enterprises, and that they are more vulnerable to internal errors and external shocks than larger organisations.

Of course, not all SMEs exist in such price-cutting environments but might still encounter degrees of resource poverty at different times, as may many larger businesses. Lacking resources in terms of legitimacy as an employer (Williamson, 2000), knowledge and money (Marlow and Patton, 1993; Klaas *et al.*, 2000), or even just sufficient headcount to complete all the tasks required in the time available, may create particular people-management challenges. SMEs can find themselves subject to their environments – for example, dependent on a single client or handful of customers who can exploit this relationship to gain very favourable terms of business. The SME, without surplus resources to help reduce such dependence, may get stuck taking these unfavourable terms (see Rainnie, 1985; Swart and Kinnie, 2003). Similarly, in relation to regulation (see Chapter 7), some have suggested that SMEs cannot cope with the 'burden' of employment regulation, in part because they lack dedicated HR staff to ensure compliance.

Elsewhere the resource challenges facing certain types of smaller business have been associated particularly with the 'liability of newness' (Stinchcombe, 1965: 148). In his chapter on 'Social structure and organizations' in James G. March's classic edited text on studying organisations, Stinchcombe considers that new organisations must overcome challenges in terms of being reliant on general skills to achieve organisational outcomes rather than skills tailored specifically to organisational needs. Furthermore, he argues, it takes time for the particular ways of working required in the organisation to become established routines and for the interpersonal relationships between organisational members to develop. Reflecting on these particular challenges we might consider how entrepreneurial and growth-oriented SMEs might struggle even after the start-up phase to obtain the sorts of knowledge and skills required to grow the business, and also the disruption caused by breaks in routines and taking on additional staff. Of course, we must not conflate size and newness (Baum, 1996), but Stinchcombe nevertheless provides a valuable way for us to think about the implications of limited resources for some SMEs.

Identifying these stylised characteristics of smaller firms allows us to develop our broad-brushstroke understanding of SMEs and helps us to mark out in this first chapter the general territory of this book. We are not suggesting that all SMEs, and no larger firms, will display high degrees of informality, close spatial and social proximity and resource poverty. Rather, these characteristics are often associated with SMEs and they have important implications for understanding employment relationships and practices in SMEs. We aim to build an approach that takes SMEs on their own terms and in context, but we see organisations as facing some common types of problem so, while we use terms such as 'recruitment and selection', 'training and development' that might be associated with formal HRM, we are interested in how SMEs adopt a 'functional equivalent' (Ram, 1999: 18) approach to address these issues on their own terms.

If understandings of HRM derived from typically larger and more formal organisations (Baron, 2003) cannot necessarily apply to explain the employment experience of SMEs, how can we make sense of and understand employment practices and relationships in these firms? Fortunately, the past 40 years or so have seen a burgeoning focus on employment relationships and practices in SMEs and, through our approach in this book, we aim to capture these developments and provide insights into the topic.

## Our approach

In this book we aim to take SMEs on their own terms. By this we mean that we will seek to understand their employment relationships and practices in light of factors such as their operating context. This perspective is about *not* constantly comparing SMEs against some supposed ideal or set of best practices derived from much larger businesses. Instead, it is about attempting to understand the situations facing SMEs and asking whether their employment relationships and practices make sense in these contexts.

As we explore different aspects of employment relationships and practices in SMEs we will draw on research literature, our own research experiences and prompt you to reflect on your own experiences and views. We will combine discussion of topics such as recruitment and selection with conceptual considerations of employment relationships in SMEs, relating this to how they are often studied and understood. This means that each of the following chapters has a dual purpose of explaining particular areas of practice and highlighting some underlying themes on the shape of employment relationships in SMEs.

### *The distinctive case of SMEs*

*Chapter 2: from entrepreneur to owner-manager*

This chapter will discuss the place of entrepreneurs in the context of the difficult change from the start-up phase to running a business and managing human resources. Importantly, this involves the entrepreneur requiring a new set of skills, the need for demonstrating leadership and engaging with employment relationships. This chapter will also discuss the relevance of human resources for firms seeking growth and what this means for the firm.

*Chapter 3: shaping employment relationships in SMEs*

This chapter will establish the factors that can have a bearing on the overall context in which SMEs' employment relationships and practices are played out. This discussion will serve two purposes: (i) sensitise readers to the diversity of organisations considered as SMEs and the need for appreciating context when discussing employment in these firms; and (ii) introduce readers to the idea that the nature of these firms may make them unsuitable for a standardised HRM model (and that this is okay).

## Managing human resources

Part II will discuss the relatively informal practices associated with managing human resources in SMEs. We will also discuss how the introduction of more formal policies impacts on these practices in a dynamic way. Throughout the book, these discussions will be attentive to the heterogeneity of SMEs.

### Chapter 4: recruitment and selection

This chapter will examine how SMEs approach recruitment and selection. We will discuss the range of techniques deployed by firms and explain how these fit within the broader approach to human resource management in SMEs. However, as with other areas of research into HRM in SMEs, there is a risk of focusing on what smaller firms *do not do* (implicitly comparing them with larger firms or prescriptive HRM literature), rather than focusing on what approaches to managing human resource they *do* undertake.

### Chapter 5: training and development

Training and development can be understood fundamentally as activities through which employees gain the skills necessary to perform their key tasks. However, SMEs are commonly regarded as providing relatively little staff training and development and the chapter will consider the reasons for this view. As a general theme, smaller organisations tend to adopt informal approaches to training and development. We will highlight where these predominantly informal approaches are useful and appropriate, but also indicate where they can give rise to problems.

### Chapter 6: reward and recognition

This chapter considers the issues of reward in SMEs, along with how these enterprises recognise employee contributions and broader issues of performance management. The value of dealing with reward and recognition together is that it allows discussion of non-financial benefits and satisfaction, which have been suggested as trade-offs for lower pay. These discussions are located, necessarily, within the wider context of the employment relationship and will consider why SMEs might struggle to adopt more 'sophisticated' performance management systems, as associated with formal models of HRM. We will therefore explore more informal means of linking pay and performance. This will also provide a platform for discussing the centrality of owner-manager prerogative within SMEs and employee perceptions of justice.

*Chapter 7: staff turnover*

Staff turnover can occur for a range of reasons, including voluntary staff departure, but more often than not, the focus is placed on dismissal and particularly unfair dismissal. The topic of staff turnover is one that excites extensive discussion and is often related to debates around legal regulation of employment in SMEs. This chapter will explore staff turnover in cases of voluntary and involuntary exit, including a discussion of managing poor performance. In this context, it will also explore the influence of tribunals and forms of regulation on influencing management practices within SMEs and critique the public debates around over-regulation of employment in SMEs.

## Re-thinking HRM in SMEs

Part III will draw out key points from the detailed discussion of SME practices to consider them in terms of firm growth and performance, and to make the case for a new, critical perspective with starting points for further research.

*Chapter 8: SME growth, HRM and the role of formalisation*

This chapter considers SME change in relation to managing human resources. In the context of informal practices the chapter focuses on the formalisation of SMEs in response to the challenges of enterprise growth and to satisfy other motives. This is an important area to consider for entrepreneurs and owner-managers seeking to grow their organisations in terms of size and profitability, and the key challenges and implications will be discussed.

*Chapter 9: employment relationships and practices in SMEs*

This chapter examines the recent trend towards researching so-called 'high performance work systems' in SMEs. Reflecting on the earlier chapters in the book, we discuss the origins of this particular line of research and consider critically what it can tell us about employment relationships and practices in SMEs, along with the ways that such perspectives can be limited.

*Chapter 10: conclusion*

The final chapter draws out the key points from the text, provides an overview of the management of human resources in SMEs and looks forward to emerging challenges. It will identify and develop important characteristics common to many SMEs, what insights these characteristics provide, and how they help us to understand SMEs, their employment relationships and their practices on their own terms.

Of course, the argument presented in this book, that we should consider SMEs as heterogeneous and their employment relationships and practices on their own terms, does not represent an uncontested fact. Rather, it is our interpretation based on our own reading and research. As part of our development as researchers, a number of our fellow researchers have influenced our work. You will see the work of these scholars referred to throughout the book. Key contributions from writers such as Paul Edwards, Ruth Holliday, Susan Marlow, Al Rainnie and Monder Ram, in particular, have shaped our understanding of the field. We also draw on a range of interesting, international contributions from different economies to help develop a wider perspective than may be available from citing a regular core of authors. Inevitably in a book of this nature, we cannot cover every piece of relevant research, nor enter into great detail on each occasion that it might prove interesting to do so. For these reasons we encourage you to read widely beyond the contents of our book. The more you read and the more widely you read, the quicker you will develop your knowledge of the topics and form your own views on the employment relationships and practices of SMEs. This book is intended to serve as a useful starting point.

In addition to our academic influences, we should also highlight the importance of practitioners in helping to shape our understanding of the issues addressed in this book. From family members and friends who have founded businesses, our professional experiences of working in small businesses, not to mention extended periods of researching SMEs and their employees, we draw on a wide range of direct and indirect experiences of SMEs and working life within them. Throughout the book we draw on examples from these businesses to illustrate particular learning points.

## Who is this book for?

This book will draw upon the growing body of international research on entrepreneurship, HRM, employment relationships and SMEs, as well as a broad range of illustrative empirical examples to provide a comprehensive review of current scholarly thinking on the topic in an accessible and engaging way. The overall objective of this text is to provide students and teachers with a resource that gives an overview of the management of human resources and employment relationships in SMEs. Mainstream textbooks on HRM pay little, if any, attention to understanding SMEs, implying that practices and processes are universally applicable. Treating SMEs as 'little big firms' (Welsh and White, 1981) in this way risks creating misunderstanding of employment issues in these enterprises and how practitioners might approach them. Similarly, entrepreneurship textbooks rarely consider how employment relationships and managing people on an everyday basis impacts upon entrepreneurs' ventures. Ignoring or misunderstanding the issues associated with the employment relationship necessarily hinders understanding of an important aspect of enterprises and of working lives.

# 2 From entrepreneur to owner-manager

The demands of not only starting but building a business commonly invoke the independence, risk taking and dynamism associated with entrepreneurs. However, it can be argued that as enterprises grow, mature and become more established, the role of everyday business management requires a different set of skills, or areas of emphasis, from those associated with a start-up. This chapter focuses on the challenging transformation from the start-up phase to the everyday management of a business with employees. Importantly, this involves adapting to the demands placed upon an owner-manager, the need for demonstrating leadership and for engaging with employment relationships.

## Entrepreneur to employer

Of the 5 million enterprises classified as SMEs within the UK economy, approximately 4 million are individuals trading on their own, without employees. As we will discuss, there is a range of reasons why these businesses, and other small enterprises with employees already, may not want to hire new staff. However, in terms of employment rates and economic prosperity, it is understandable that governments might want to target the self-employed, one-person enterprises and encourage them to take on employees. Mathematically at least, if every one-person enterprise in the UK took on one employee this would create 4 million jobs!

For example, the Federation of Small Businesses, 'the UK's *largest campaigning pressure group* promoting and protecting the interests of the self-employed and owners of small firms' (FSB, 2015, emphasis in original), argued in a report on the role of small businesses in employment and enterprise that:

> Our analysis suggests that 74 per cent of those we observe becoming self-employed with employees come from the self-employed who previously had no employees, while a further 13 per cent come from the ranks of employees in micro-businesses. Individuals making this transition are therefore a particularly important part of the entrepreneurial pipeline and generator of jobs. In light of the evidence ... we would argue that supporting self-employed individuals to take on an employee is a highly

important – and arguably overlooked – means of helping the unemployed and non-participants get back into work. This may also widen access to entrepreneurship.

(Urwin and Buscha, 2012: 9)

However, none of this is straightforward. While many governments work hard at limiting the obstacles to employing new staff and to encourage a growth mindset among business owners, small businesses tend not to grow beyond their initial size and very few could be considered 'high growth' (see Storey, 2011). While there is a broad range of reasons why small businesses do not grow into medium-sized or large businesses, Sloan and Chittenden (2006), among others like Scase and Goffee (1987), offer evidence suggesting that the appetite for growth may be limited. We return to this discussion later in this chapter in the section 'Assumptions of growth'.

For those who do want to grow their employee numbers, for example a start-up enterprise or growth-oriented entrepreneurs, they must engage with a number of steps. Formally, in taking on a first employee the business owner will have to comply with specific legal requirements. In the UK, for example, new employers are advised to:

1 Decide how much to pay an employee (complying with national minimum wage legislation).
2 Confirm that the proposed recruit has the legal right to work in the UK.
3 Conduct background checks on a potential employee's criminal record and suitability for certain roles, such as those requiring security clearance or caring for vulnerable people.
4 Obtain employers' liability insurance.
5 Prepare and send details of the job, including terms and conditions, to the employee.
6 Register as an employer with the tax authorities.

(www.gov.uk/employing-staff)

Beyond these immediate legal issues, moving from self-employment or as part of a start-up team can give rise to numerous other considerations and challenges. Whether businesses are able to cope with these challenges, and how they cope with them, may influence the success of the business and how it develops.

### Task 2.1

Moving from being a self-employed, one-person enterprise to becoming an employer will give rise to numerous fresh considerations for the business owner, especially in respect of the employment relationship. Focus on the context of an economy that interests you and try to map out as many of these challenges as you can think of.

## The challenges of moving from entrepreneur to owner-manager

Taking on employees creates fresh challenges for entrepreneurs and in this section we begin to characterise the nature of these different pressures. The transition to becoming an owner-manager and of having to engage with the challenges associated with human resource management have been noted by some commentators as one of the key obstacles to establishing a business, and that 'an inability on the part of some founders of new ventures to successfully manage HRM issues is an important factor in their ultimate failure' (Baron, 2003: 253). The key challenges can be broadly considered in terms of resources, delegation and skills.

### Resources

The first pressure likely to strike the small business owner is the added costs within their business. Growth requires resources and, for employment growth, this creates demands on finances, time and management effort such that appointing a new employee and getting them to a point where they can make a contribution to the business can prove tougher than may be initially thought. The considerations of taking on a new employee extend beyond whether the business can afford their salary.

As a founder and director at a communications firm explained to us:

> in taking people on it's always about the balance of risk and reward. You know, you're committed to pay them a certain amount, which puts pressure on the business to earn more money.
>
> And of course, if you're new in business you forget about that. Well we don't now ... when you learn, you learn about the actual true cost of employing somebody. And the true commitment of employing someone is very different than just what it looks like in the advert, 20,000 a year. By the time they've got holidays, insurance, pensions, you know all those kind of things ...

A quick Internet search for guidance on the typical costs of employment for an employee returns a wide range of estimates. Issues around additional computing equipment and IT licences required, training provision and employment-related benefits can all influence the costs beyond a basic salary. Using one online calculator suggests that an employee earning £25,000 gross annual salary will cost the business over £42,000, subject to certain assumptions being made about benefits and, of course, not taking into account the additional income that employee can *generate* for the business which should at least cover these employment costs.

The considerations of hiring a new employee extend beyond these types of financial resource implications. For example, the founder director also revealed the precarious nature of resourcing particular projects or contracts as well as some sense of a moral dimension in the decision to employ a member of staff. He felt that businesses owe it to their employees not to engage in 'hire and fire' practices as business demand fluctuates:

> it's a big risk to take, you know, one's always in the stage of 'can you deliver?' or do you want to be in a position where you can deliver it before you pitch for [work]? So that dilemma is always facing us. As we've recruited, we are becoming more inclined to ... go towards contracts once we've got a base amount of people because, I don't mean this ruthlessly, you take on a big burden when you employ someone full time.
>
> And also I think there's a moral dimension as well, that it's a fluid business. You could take someone on and then in a few months' time you could be saying 'goodbye' to them because there isn't enough work. Well at least we're being straight and up front with people, you know, 'we'll give you a contract and it's a rolling contract' and that seems to be an emerging position at the moment.

While this business may have overcome the challenge of staff recruitment, how can an owner-manager keep the business operating or growing as they incorporate new employees and new ways of working? Taking time away from hands-on activities that earn money for the business today in order to ensure new staff know how to develop the business and generate income into the future may be especially challenging for owners who are closely involved with earning money for the business (see Cardon and Stevens, 2004). While, during a start-up phase, this kind of direct owner-manager involvement in all aspects of the business may be necessary to ensure quality and control costs, such intensive involvement in all aspects of the business cannot be sustained as the enterprise grows. This will require degrees of delegation.

### *Delegation*

As a start-up transitions into the day-to-day running of a business, entrepreneurs can find the accompanying change in their roles and responsibilities challenging – moving from the excitement of building a new venture towards something requiring more traditional management and monitoring. Perhaps one of the biggest challenges in this regard is that of delegation (Churchill and Lewis, 1983). Delegation involves handing certain tasks over to another person so that they can undertake the work required. In this way, rapid growth and fast-changing management structures can create opportunities for career-advancement and skill acquisition not available in more rigidly hierarchical large firms. However, learning to delegate can pose difficulties for business owners who are accustomed to making decisions alone and implementing them as they see fit (Charan et al., 1980). Reluctance to release some control to others in the business or to accept that established projects and practices may be loss making can create tensions. Employees might resent constraints and interference (Packham et al., 2005) while owners' strong adherence to pet projects or views can hold back the business and drain resources (Patzelt et al., 2008).

When we discussed this process with Jane, the owner of several successful enterprises, she revealed that her passion was in creating start-up ventures rather than what she saw as the more mundane aspects of managing and monitoring performance over time. Jane's response to this was to step away from daily involvement in her newest venture and hand it over to managers who oversaw related parts of the broader business. However, we also talked to some of Jane's employees and, for them, this change was difficult to accept:

> it is a bit disheartening because I have gone from a point where Jane says to me 'I am going to give you the business, you run it as you wish'. I have been doing that for a year and a half. And now [under the business manager] it is a case of being told: 'I need you sat where I can see you. I need you to take your lunch at this time. I need you to call me if you are going to be late. You sacrifice your break even if you are doing work'. It has gone from being an integral part of the start-up to being an employee. And I could be an employee elsewhere for a lot more money. And one thing that we often say actually is, and we wouldn't want to do it, but what we are doing right now we could be doing in my front living room, me and my colleague. We could essentially be setting up a business doing exactly what we are doing on two laptops in one of our front rooms. We are here because we want to work for Jane and we want to work with Jane.

Reaching the stage at which work is gladly handed over to an employee can take time for an owner who has traditionally worked alone and may have started a venture for the apparent independence it offers. While there might be some intention to recruit staff who can be trained in the skills and approaches to work that the owner-manager prefers, research by Packham et al., (2005) suggests that this is easier said than done. Packham and his colleagues conducted group interviews with SME owner-managers in Wales about their perceptions of the development of management skills and practices within their firms. All the participants in their study felt that management development was intertwined with growth decisions but some reported problems delegating due to a lack of belief in the ability of existing staff to rise to the challenge.

Common to accounts of owner-managers in SMEs, there was a reluctance to introduce formal systems to support delegation and management because they were seen as bureaucratic and inappropriate for their business. Within this context, owner-managers might prefer the apparently simpler route of recruiting employees who can make a practical contribution straightaway. Such an approach is not quite as simple as it may appear and, in Packham et al.'s study, this approach was viewed as entailing difficulties not only in recruiting but also retaining those staff who already had the required management skills.

In light of these challenges it might be understandable when some entrepreneurs conduct the management of their firm through a 'key employee' as they start up new ventures. Work by Schlosser (2014, 2015) in Canada details how entrepreneurs may rely on a particular employee who they perceive as effective, reliable and with whom they have enough shared history for them to be deemed trustworthy. In this way, trust, willingly making oneself vulnerable to another (Rousseau et al., 1998), can be an important element in the decisions of owner-managers of relatively informal, unstructured businesses. These trusted and so-called key employees can reduce some of the uncertainties associated with entering a new business venture as well as free the business owner from the challenges of day-to-day staff management. Consequently, Schlosser (2015) indicates, key employees might accompany an entrepreneur through multiple start-up ventures, providing some sense of security for the business owner.

## Skills

For an owner-manager whose venture is becoming an established business with employees, this places an emphasis on a different set of skills from those that might have proven useful in getting the venture off the ground (Coad et al., 2013). In addition to the psychological step of relinquishing some control over part of the business, as an employer the business owner will have to develop the skills of giving clear instructions and, perhaps, learning to accommodate ways of working different from their own. Similar to difficulties in delegating to staff they do not fully trust with their business operations, sometimes an owner-manager can grow frustrated by employees' apparent inability to anticipate what they want done.

Recounting a recently held team meeting with two new starters, the owner-manager of a recruitment firm told us about his exasperation at these staff not knowing about a particular 'Star Job' feature on the company website. When asked to clarify whether he had alerted the new starters to this feature, he responded simply that new staff 'don't show any initiative', perhaps implying that he had not shown them. On this and other occasions, the owner-manager struggled to come to terms with the relative lack of investment from employees who, rather than sharing his love of the business, worked for their pay cheques. This difference of view is perhaps understandable given that he was the sole owner of the business and his employees were focused on their own careers and ambitions.

Managing as an employer also impacts how the entrepreneur conducts themselves in the business on a day-to-day basis. While self-employed, a business owner is largely accountable only to their external clients but, with employees, an owner-manager can also find themselves 'on show' even when not in front of clients. For example, as we discuss in Chapter 6, important in many areas of the employment relationship are perceptions of procedural justice – that employees are treated fairly and without favouritism or prejudice. This new element of scrutiny can place demands on the owner-manager's conduct, especially when it is seen to vary from what is required of employees or the image projected externally to clients.

Within the context of an owner-manager introducing new timesheets and a renewed focus on people's timekeeping at a growth-oriented small firm that we worked with, one employee reported his frustration at seeing the owner and his girlfriend arrive well after the start of the usual working day with no acknowledgement or offer of an explanation. The owner-manager was working by far the longest hours in the business and he was trying to regain some degree of work-life balance by making staff more accountable for their output. However, by not clearly communicating his justifications for reducing his own hours while requiring timesheets from employees, the owner-manager was open to charges of hypocrisy. The skills involved in managing these types of issue are a long way from the external focus of business start-up and may not be what a new owner-manager expects or is prepared for.

In general terms, owner-managers can be confronted by a lack of know-how concerning aspects of managing employees (Churchill and Lewis, 1983). As Cardon and Stevens (2004) point out, certain aspects of managing staff may arise somewhat infrequently. Owner-managers may, for example, be ill-practised in how to motivate employees in a given situation, identify particular training needs or, perhaps, discipline or dismiss someone. Such knowledge and skills can, of course, be acquired as necessary but, as Beckman and Burton (2008) report, those businesses founded by people with a narrow experience base of a particular function can sometimes struggle to appreciate the value of other functions. There has to be caution in assuming that an owner-manager will somehow intuitively know when to take appropriate advice about managing employment relationships in their business.

### Task 2.2

Imagine you are running a business and have recently taken on your first employees.

1. How would you acquire the best ways of managing your employees? Try to be as specific as possible on the kinds of sources you might draw on. (Hint: do not forget popular representations of entrepreneurs and managers portrayed in the media as a source of information.)
2. Discuss each source with your colleagues and rate each in terms of how accessible the source is and how likely it is you think each source would provide useful information.

## From entrepreneur to owner-manager?

The challenges associated with moving from being a self-employed business owner to an owner-manager with employees have been characterised as a transition from entrepreneur to owner-manager. This perspective has, however, been criticised as 'dangerous and misleading' when it comes to understanding management in small businesses (Watson, 1995: 35). These criticisms suggest that the perspective over-simplifies how businesses develop in three main respects: assumptions of growth, the challenge of change, and the underlying 'from/to' logic of this perspective. We consider each of these in turn.

## Assumptions of growth

We started this chapter by identifying how governments are attracted to the idea of boosting employment in small firms given what this can achieve for reducing unemployment figures and, potentially, growth in gross domestic product (GDP). However, we must not assume that all self-employed people, or even all small firms, want to take on more employees (Scase and Goffee, 1982; Sloan and Chittenden, 2006). Caution is required, then, when faced with suggestions that the self-employed or the small firm are at the start of a pathway towards growth.

Taking on a first employee can represent a major step for many and it is a step that some would rather avoid. Some may view becoming an employer as hampering the independence they sought when becoming self-employed (Scase and Goffee, 1982). This is a thought we have found echoed in our own research:

> what you tend to find is that while you have this sort of passion and commitment and all that sort of stuff, staff generally don't ... You know, now I don't really want all that hassle and aggravation that staff give you really.

Opting for self-employment or to run a small business may frequently be driven simply by a desire to earn a living rather than the first step on the path to building a larger business. For some, this represents a lifestyle choice, and such 'lifestyle businesses' have been defined as 'those providing an income for the household or family and not having a growth orientation' (Fletcher, 2010: 454). While fulfilling important functions in the economy in terms of employment provision and providing income to owners and any employees, lifestyle businesses have tended to be overlooked relative to the attention granted to growth-oriented enterprises. However, labelling lifestyle businesses as 'trundlers' (Storey, 1994: 119) or 'static' (see Burns and Harrison, 1996: 41) risks misrepresenting the nature of these businesses and therefore limiting understanding of an important element of the economy (Bennett, 2014).

Moreover, growing a business can be achieved without additional employees, for example by increasing financial turnover from existing operations or using subcontractors to increase capacity (Bischoff and Wood, 2013). This suggests that 'growth' is not a particularly helpful concept without qualification and that 'non-growth' might actually be 'different growth' in certain cases. Nevertheless, there remains a persistent view that most small businesses harbour ambitions to grow. This style of 'acorns-to-oaks' thinking (Weatherill and Cope, 1969) has been challenged in detail by Gray (1998) on the basis that it views small businesses as generally growth oriented and destined to pass through specific stages of growth. In contrast, Gray highlights evidence suggesting that the motivations behind starting and running a business frequently do not include ambitions to grow or hire more employees. Moreover, among those businesses that do pursue or achieve growth, it is often with a view to achieving a particular end, such as to sell off the business as a going concern, rather than as an ongoing pursuit of growth for its own sake.

Gray's analysis highlights an apparent tension between politicians' objectives and those of small business owners. As MacDonald *et al.* (2007: 78) have commented:

> Where SMEs are involved, perhaps the crucial link is between policy of any sort and cold reality. For instance, a simplistic view of SMEs is still common among policy makers who are capable of seeing SMEs simply as nascent large firms that should be exploiting innovation to realize their growth potential. SMEs, it would seem, have no business being small.

Yet, despite such refutations, assumptions accompanying acorns-to-oaks thinking still remains commonplace today – a topic we will return to in Chapter 8.

## The challenge of change

A further criticism associated with the transitions businesses are assumed to undergo relates to the ease with which change may be implemented. Writing on the related theme of changing management styles, Charan *et al.*'s (1980) widely cited paper, 'From entrepreneurial to professional management: a set of guidelines', presents a step-by-step approach to the transition.

Charan *et al.*'s starting point is that to continue growing, small businesses must successfully navigate 'a transition from an entrepreneurial to a professionally managed system' (Charan *et al.*, 1980: 1). Within the ordered framework presented, the business owner first recognises a need to change their working practices, before conducting analysis on how the business currently operates. In subsequent steps the business owner decides on a new formal structure which is implemented gradually, complemented by the training of suitable middle managers. This process, according to Charan *et al.*, culminates in a revised organisation structure that allows an owner to delegate decision making, enable decisions to be made on the basis of data and to avoid over-reliance on particular individuals.

Although Charan *et al.* acknowledge the potential difficulties associated with aspects of these stages, there remains an underlying sense of a step-by-step map towards successful organisational change. The result is that the change process is over-simplified with limited consideration given to tricky issues such as whether the entrepreneur can recognise the need to change in the first place and accept that some response is required. Further, Jayawarna et al., (2013) identify that motivations may change over the course of time in a business, highlighting that the business environment is not necessarily constant – the kinds of approaches and solutions that worked at one point might become unsuited to the enterprise in terms of environment, goals or the consequences of previous decisions.

Adapting the work of Miller (1992), we can start to understand how difficult it can be for an entrepreneur to recognise that change in their approach may be required. Miller has described the 'Icarus paradox' to help explain why successful organisations might not see a need to change what they are doing. The Icarus story from Greek mythology is well known: Icarus and his father Daedalus were being held prisoner on an island, so Daedalus created some wings to help them fly away to freedom. The wings were made of wax and feathers so, before they made their bid for escape, Daedalus warned his son not to fly too close to the sea or the sun. The plan was a success, with Icarus using these wings to soar away from the prison, until, carried away with his new-found ability, he wanted to go further and higher and he continued to climb, taking him towards the sun. Closer to the sun's warmth, the wax holding Icarus's wings started to melt. Melted wax wings do not work very well and, while Icarus could defy his erstwhile captor King Minos, the same could not be said for gravity. Icarus fell from the sky to a watery fate.

The point of this story, as Miller sees it, is that organisations can bring about their eventual downfall by continuing to do the things that have made them successful to date. Miller breaks down the Icarus paradox into two main issues: (i) success can lead to failure; and (ii) actions that lead to success at one time do not *always* lead to success.

The first point is quite simply to highlight the risk posed by hubris, brought on by success. In Miller's (1992: 31) own words, 'Icarus flew so well that he got cocky and overambitious'. The same can be said of some businesses where early success can lead them to underestimate the challenges of a competitive environment or new product launch. The second point is described as being 'too much of a good thing' (ibid.: 31), and is explained as organisations extending practices that they believe have made them successful to the point of dysfunction. For example, a business that attributes a large degree of its success to careful planning may come to be overly rigid by seeking to plan every last detail. In the case of a small business, it could be that the business enjoys early success through a profitable contract with a single supplier but, over time, the business tailors its operations increasingly to meeting the wishes of that client such that it loses the ability to diversify its client base and grow. Dependent on a single client, a small business may find itself subject to the demands and decisions of that client (Rainnie, 1989).

At the heart of Miller's analysis is the idea that organisations exist in dynamic environments and must, therefore, remain dynamic to account for changes in that environment. Simply repeating the practices associated with prior success may reflect that a business is not seeking to adapt to environmental changes. In the case of the entrepreneur who takes on employees, they might remain wedded to their original vision for the business (Beckman and Burton, 2008) and preferred ways of working, while failing to spot when the skills required to start a business should be altered in favour of the skills to manage it on an ongoing basis (Breslin, 2010).

Phelps *et al.* (2007) suggest that businesses will change their management structures when the problems caused by existing practices are thought to outweigh the risks of adopting new practices. As we will discuss in greater detail in Chapter 8, however, identifying these 'tipping points' while in the midst of day-to-day business operations can represent a significant challenge for busy owner-managers (Mallett and Wapshott, 2014), and many may find themselves too close to the heat of the sun, failing to adapt to their changing circumstances.

## The underlying 'from/to' logic of this perspective

Watson (1995), whose paper 'Entrepreneurship and professional management: a fatal distinction' prompted us to include this section of the chapter, presents an interesting and detailed consideration of how businesses change as they grow, and criticises the underlying logic of a transition 'from' one state 'to' another. He argues that such an approach to understanding how businesses develop risks distracting attention from the ways in which all businesses need to consider an appropriate balance of creativity and innovation with operational control. Watson's point is that by adopting the 'from/to' logic of the transition perspective, we may come to misunderstand how both small and large businesses operate.

Criticising the 'naïve evolutionism' (Watson, 1995: 35) of perspectives that imply one stage of development is left behind as a new business form replaces the old, Watson suggests that there can be significant overlap in the management orientations found in both small and large businesses. Each may require, albeit to differing degrees, entrepreneurial and more traditional management behaviours if they are to be successful in coping with the challenges presented by their competitive environments. Importantly, the establishment and ongoing management of a small firm does not remove the need for entrepreneurial creativity and innovation, but neither can the increasing pressures of employment relationships and management tasks within the firm be ignored.

While we cannot assume that all owner-managers will want to grow their businesses and that the processes of change may be simple or linear, there remains a different set of challenges and potentially different skills required when deciding to take on employees. For example, this may relate to recruitment and selection, training and development, reward and recognition, or staff exit – the core topics covered in this book. The 'from entrepreneur to owner-manager' transition might better be understood as a series of questions and decisions that the owner(s) must address as their business, and its relationship to the wider operating environment, changes. How (and if) these questions and decisions are addressed will shape the business and the employment relationships within it (Levie and Lichtenstein, 2010).

## Conclusion

In this chapter we have highlighted how entrepreneurship is not solely concerned with business start-up. If a business wants to grow, or indeed does grow, this often entails getting to grips with managing employees and a range of new demands such as generating sufficient resources to pay employees and learning to delegate in order to make the most of the people employed.

The challenges associated with a shift from being a self-employed business owner to an owner-manager with employees have been characterised as a transition from entrepreneur to owner-manager. This perspective has, however, been criticised as misleading and even as dangerous when it comes to understanding management in small businesses, because it risks over-simplifying the ways in which businesses develop. This over-simplification can be considered in respect to assumptions of growth, the challenge of change and the underlying 'from/to' logic of this perspective.

The key point to take from this chapter is that managing a small business can present different challenges or require different emphases compared with the start-up of a new venture. To overcome these challenges, entrepreneurs may require new skills and knowledge, some brand new, others a change in style depending on the starting point of their business and considerations such as the operating environment, knowledge that relates to the topics covered in this book. In the next chapter we start to consider in greater detail the factors facing SMEs that can shape or influence the employment relationships and practices we associate with these enterprises.

# 3 Shaping employment relationships in SMEs

## Introduction

This chapter will broadly trace the history of research into the management of human resources in SMEs, drawing out the key debates around the opposition between a 'small is beautiful' approach and a 'bleak house' approach to understanding employment relationships in these firms. These debates are placed within the important political context which has often had a close relationship with research that is both influenced by it and, at times, reacts in opposition to particular political assumptions or agendas. We will then discuss the different factors, both external and internal to the firm, that shape SMEs' employment relationships and the ways in which these factors interact. This attention to the different influences on SMEs allows us, building on the work of Gilman and Edwards (2008), to develop an approach to understanding and studying the implications of the heterogeneity of these businesses.

## The political creation of the small firm

Over the past 40 years dominant representations of entrepreneurship and SMEs have positioned them as routes towards economic prosperity for both individuals and nations (see, for example, Young 1992, 2013). Such meanings are not static, however, and Dannreuther and Perren (2013a) examine how small firms have been talked about and are defined within political debate. They suggest that the idea of the small firm can be talked about in a variety of different ways, and used to support different political ends, because it is 'transient and contested, varying by place, time and political purpose' (ibid.: 1). How small firms have been thought about, defined and regulated has changed over time, and Dannreuther and Perren's book traces this process and the subsequent exploitation of the labels 'small firm' and 'SME' through an historical analysis of political debate. Their analysis identifies three key eras: 1803–1969, the era of the shopkeeper and exclusion of the small firm; 1970–80, the construction of the small firm; and 1980–2004, the exploitation of this small firm construct.

The authors demonstrate how prior to the 1970s, the small firm was largely excluded from political debate. An exception was the occasional mention of shopkeepers, for example in debates around post-war rationing, but these were still relatively small in number. There were, of course, exceptions, such as in the John Maynard Keynes-authored Macmillan Committee report which highlighted problems for small firms in accessing finance (Macmillan, 1931). However, small firms were generally more a concern of local politics, and 'small firm' as a category lacked definition and forms of voice and representation, especially in a context of increasing centralisation and government coordination. During this time the political significance of small firms and their exclusion was in epitomising 'the traditional, parochial, exploitative and inefficient economy that the modernisers sought to eradicate' (Dannreuther and Perren, 2013a: 96).

When small firms did eventually emerge in political debate in the 1960s it was in becoming part of a larger debate around closing tax loop holes, and small firms were identified as particularly vulnerable to tax (Bolton, 1971). This emergence of a particular conception of what defines a small firm in the context of particular political agendas had (and continues to have) important implications for SME research, including that on employment relationships and practices within these firms.

## Small is beautiful

The emergence of a prominent conception of small and medium-sized enterprises as distinct from larger firms and of importance in their own right occurred at the beginning of the 1970s. This was, in part, prompted by a shift in the business population where small firms were seen to be in decline while the numbers of businesses employing more than 200 people were increasing (Fuller, 2003). In response, the Bolton Committee was appointed in 1969 to assess small firms' role in the UK economy and make recommendations on improving government policy and support, to address a perceived problem that 'the formulation of industrial policy has inevitably proceeded without adequate knowledge of small firms' (Bolton, 1971: xv).

In an important way, as Dannreuther and Perren (2013a, 2013b) suggest, this report effectively created the small firm and, as Fuller (2003: 306) has argued:

> from its outset, the political definition of small business, and, I would argue its subsequent cultural meaning in the UK and many western cultures, was dialectically grounded in the existence of large business.

The second era Dannreuther and Perren identify in their analysis of political debate therefore traces the subsequent explosion of interest and political establishment of the small firm, centred on the Bolton Committee and its 1971 report. This technocratic-led committee was formed from the eventual emergence of a voice for small businesses, in the form of the Confederation of British Industry (CBI), and louder calls for revision of the tax system. This increasing attention and pressure led to the creation of an independent inquiry to be focused predominantly on helping dynamic, innovative small firms.

The Bolton Committee accordingly produced a functionalist definition of the small firm in its terms of reference, focused on market share and sectoral considerations of size as opposed to any absolute or standard measure of employee numbers or turnover. This ensured its practical utility, adopting a '200 employee upper limit for manufacturing and a series of more or less arbitrary definitions in terms of whatever measures appear appropriate for other trades' (Bolton, 1971: 2). That is, the committee adopted definitions that related most usefully to existing statistical sources owing to a lack of comprehensive records.

Clearly, the report acknowledges the heterogeneity of SMEs, although it goes on to suggest (Bolton, 1971: xv) that what gives unity and meaning to the concept of the small firm is that they have owner-managers and tend to lack formal management structures and trade unions. The choice of employee size limits for different sectors was therefore chosen not only due to statistical utility but also to fit with these characteristics. For example, in manufacturing, a given number of employees may work for a manufacturing firm at a single location with greater direct management intervention from the owner than is possible in a geographically disperse chain of retail stores with the same number of employees.

For Dannreuther and Perren, the work of the Bolton Committee was heavily influenced by the agendas of the political elite, legitimising the CBI as a representative voice of small business and framing these firms in terms of their contribution to the wider economy. This had little relation to many small firms, such as those locally focused, lifestyle or family firms far removed from the CBI or wider political concerns. The conception of the small firm that was produced was a romanticised one in line with this ungrounded political viewpoint, picturing small firms as entrepreneurial and fundamentally independent. This was brought about through a focus on the owner-managers and a generalising assumption that SME owner-manager motivations involved freedom and independence.

In their overview of the report ten years later, Curran and Stanworth (1982: 4) describe the lack of engagement with employment relationships or employees more generally:

> [T]he Report showed that small firms employed a substantial proportion of the labour force – over 30 per cent of the workers in the industries covered by the enquiry (Bolton Report, 1971: 33). Yet not a single piece of research directly investigated employer-employee relations or employee reactions to employment in the small firm. The Committee's two principal surveys enquiring into the characteristics of small firms in Britain achieved response rates of only 13 and 22 per cent and most of the various research reports make little attempt to claim to be more than preliminary studies.

Importantly for our focus, the Bolton Committee's romanticised view compared the working environment of small firms favourably with that found in large industrial employers, many of which were experiencing troubles at the time. The report identified positives such as closer working relationships, flexibility, role variety and opportunities to develop, as well as other conveniences such as location, suggesting that these advantages offset the lower rates of pay than those found in larger firms (Bolton, 1971: 21). There was a (perhaps naïve) assumption that if employees were willing to work for low pay they must be compensated in other ways.

While it built on earlier work (for example, Revans, 1956), the report is frequently cited as helping to foster this harmonious view of working life in small firms (Baines and Wheelock, 1998; Dundon et al., 1999) and the phrase 'small is beautiful' was applied to describe this perspective (Schumacher, 1973; Holliday, 1995). This standpoint is particularly important to understand because, as Curran and Stanworth (1982) explain, the report's 'findings and recommendations have formed the bedrock of virtually all research, analysis and policy making since' (Curran and Stanworth, 1982: 3).

As Bolton outlines, and has been regularly cited (see for example, Storey, 1994; Wilkinson, 1999):

> In many respects a small firm provides a better environment for the employee than is possible in most large firms ... Each employee is also likely to have a more varied role with a chance to participate in several kinds of work ... no doubt as a result ... turnover of staff in small firms is very low and strikes and other kinds of industrial dispute are relatively infrequent.
>
> (Bolton, 1971: 21)

As well as building on earlier work such as that of Revans (1956), who identified, for example, lower rates of absenteeism and industrial action in smaller organisations, the Bolton Committee Report also chimed with contemporary academic research. An important example is the work of Ingham (1970), whose PhD study of the Bradford (UK) engineering sector during the mid-1960s became the widely discussed text *Size of Industrial Organization & Worker Behaviour*. In this work Ingham argued that greater intrinsic rewards were received in smaller firms through greater involvement and focus on particular work tasks and stronger social relationships. These intrinsic motivations, produced by the informal, close working environments of many smaller firms, were argued to lead to an alternative form of job satisfaction to the relatively higher paying, extrinsic rewards of larger firms:

> In short, it was shown that the large plant workers were *economistic* and *instrumental* in their orientation to work; that is they were very sensitive to the economic (especially wages) aspects of their employment and less concerned with non-economic factors. On the other hand, the small firm men appeared to be setting their acceptable wage level at a much lower level and, at the same time, demanded a higher level of non-economic rewards (*non-economistic/expressive* orientation).
>
> (Ingham, 1970: 143, emphasis in original)

In forming their conclusions, the Bolton Committee overlooked the alternative ways, beyond strikes and formal industrial action, that discontent may be demonstrated in the workplace. For example, subtle forms of resistance such as minor fiddles or 'sickness' absence might serve to signal displeasure with management actions or claim some kind of redress (Rainnie, 1989). The Bolton Committee's use of measures more appropriate to large firms, such as the occurrence of strikes as a measure of employee satisfaction, neglects not only these alternative expressions of discontent but also to consider the generally lower degree of unionisation found in smaller firms. This problem of misunderstanding small firms through the application of measures and approaches applied to understand large firms will become a common theme as we discuss a variety of studies throughout this book.

Despite these significant limitations in the committee's report, Dannreuther and Perren demonstrate how its construction of the small firm was eagerly taken up by politicians. Subsequently, the third era Dannreuther and Perren identify, from 1980 onwards, involves the subsequent 'invention, capture and exploitation of this idealised constituency' (Dannreuther and Perren, 2013a: 130). These ways of thinking about small firms have been deployed by different political agendas, from the individualism of Margaret Thatcher to the proposed inclusion and social justice of New Labour. Politically, small firms have therefore become viewed as central to Britain's knowledge-based, liberal market economy and part of an increasingly broad range of political debate, with similar impacts and implications internationally.

## Bleak house

Despite its political value, the 'small is beautiful' perspective of harmonious working relationships in small firms was challenged through academic work by researchers such as Curran and Stanworth (1981), Rainnie (1989), Goss (1991) and Scase (1995), who drew attention to the poor employment conditions present in some small businesses and the limited alternative choices in the labour market for those working within them. We will return to Rainnie's influential text and his broader work later in this chapter.

Curran and Stanworth (1981) conducted interviews with 118 shop-floor workers in eight small firms in the printing and electronics industries, as well as 83 comparable interviews with employees of large firms. The authors raise important issues such as that large firms, in an era when many people remained in one organisation for much of their careers, offered a wider range of tasks and development opportunities, especially when considering factors such as an employee's life stage which they describe in terms of, for example, family commitments and responsibilities. Curran and Stanworth also identified greater job autonomy and less close supervision in the larger firms, which makes sense when we think back to the first chapter's discussion of owner-managers and conditions of spatial proximity. Studies such as this cast doubt on conceptions of SMEs as providing greater or more intrinsic job satisfaction.

A more critical, alternative portrayal of working lives in some small firms has been labelled as the 'bleak house' (Sisson, 1993) vision of employment. In adopting this label, Sisson was discussing the state of industrial relations and management practices in non-unionised workplaces large and small. Drawing on data gathered from the third Workplace Industrial Relations Survey (a nation-wide British survey on workplace employment relations), Sisson suggests that without pressure from trade unions, managers are free to rule as they see fit rather than conforming to good practices or the structures and processes of HRM. This could be seen, he argued, in areas such as increasing claims of unfair dismissal. The significance of these observations is that union presence is limited in smaller business establishments (Rainnie, 1989) and Sisson therefore suggests that SMEs are less likely to adopt rigorous, negotiated management practices such as HRM.

Furthermore, Scott and Rainnie (1982: 186) discuss their research into small firms in the clothing sector as portraying a bleak picture of employment relationships:

> [T]he picture we have attempted to paint is not one of happy families watched over by paternalist owners. Rather it is a picture of autocratic management style, dictated by enormous external pressures on the owner managers themselves to cut costs. The workforce can no longer resort to frequent job changing to alleviate the conditions of work, but equally finds difficulty in undertaking collective action, except in extreme cases. This difficulty should not, we contend, be mistaken for harmony; small scale enterprises such as the clothing firms we have studied have advantages in terms of managerial control, especially if the workforce is female. They are not necessarily the 'better environment' for the worker envisaged by the Bolton Report.

Discussion of the 'small is beautiful' and 'bleak house' perspectives is necessary to understand some of the terminology used in reading about employment relationships in small firms and the labels serve a purpose of organising competing representations of these relationships. As with any characterisation, however, we need to be careful of demanding more from it than the characterisation can support. For example, a large-scale, regional UK study by Bacon et al. (1996) found a surprisingly high take-up of practices associated with HRM, casting doubt on the bleak house perspective and the assumption that those firms lacking union representation are unlikely to adopt HRM (see Edwards and Ram, 2010). If it is treated as more than a helpful way of organising alternative views, the 'small is beautiful' versus 'bleak house' characterisation can distract us from engaging in more subtle discussions of the middle ground between these poles and seeking to understand how employment relationships and practices in SMEs are shaped and enacted on an ongoing, everyday basis.

> **Task 3.1**
>
> Search the contents of reputable news sources over recent weeks. Identify a news story relating to SMEs. Consider: (i) How is the firm relevant to the story? (ii) How is the firm presented in the story? (iii) Do you think the author of the article is broadly positive, neutral or negative about SMEs in general? (iv) Based on the information in the story, would you want to work in an SME? You may wish to discuss your ideas with colleagues.

There is not one simple answer to describing employment relationships and practices in SMEs. As is no doubt becoming clear, SMEs are a highly heterogeneous grouping and to understand how their employment relationships are shaped, we need to refer to debates over what influences are operating at any given time and in varying contexts (Goss, 1991).

## Shaping employment relationships

We can approach the task of understanding what shapes employment relationships and practices in small firms by drawing out two main, related perspectives. The first perspective we characterise as 'external influences', given its attempt to highlight the role of significant external influences on how relationships within firms are conducted. The second is an 'interactions' perspective that emphasises interplay of external and internal influences to shape employment relationships and practices.

### *External influences*

Rainnie's book, *Industrial Relations in Small Firms: Small Isn't Beautiful* (1989) grew out of his wider intellectual project discussing the role of small businesses in the political and economic upheavals associated with the enterprise culture in 1980s Britain (see, for example, Rainnie, 1985). As large firms responded to financial crises, in part through fragmentation and the development of external supply chains, this created greater opportunities for the emergence and growth of small firms. Politically, small firms had been 'entrusted with part of the burden of resuscitating the crisis wracked British economy' (Rainnie, 1985: 143). Rainnie identifies a range of functions ascribed to small firms within the political philosophy of the 1980s:

1 Provide a source of competition to large firms.
2 Create new jobs.
3 Provide the seedcorn from which giant corporations will grow.
4 Provide a harmonious working environment, thus reducing strikes and absenteeism.
5 Aid in the regeneration of inner cities.
6 Provide a source of innovation.

In particular, Rainnie is concerned with challenging the kind of 'small is beautiful' image that was dominating policy discussions at the time, not just in the UK but internationally, for example in Japan and Italy. Rainnie (1985: 148) observes how the idea 'that somehow small firms can overcome the inherent antagonism between capital and labour, has sunk deep into the consciousness of academics, government and media'. In his 1989 book he therefore seeks to explain how small firms are often subject to the decisions and actions of very large businesses, especially their choices over which markets to compete in and their actions in outsourcing production. According to Rainnie, in this way large businesses exert significant influence on the opportunities for smaller firms.

Drawing on and developing Shutt and Whittington's (1987) work seeking to understand the changing role of small businesses in the UK economy, Rainnie (1989) presents a four-part classification of small firms based on their relation to large businesses:

1   Dependent: 'dependence, when it does arise, will be of fundamental importance in determining the internal structure and activity of that firm' (Rainnie, 1989: 84).
2   Competitive independent: 'lacking the resources of their large-scale opponents they survive by hyper-exploitation either of labour or of fixed capital, or most probably both' (Rainnie, 1989: 84).
3   Old independent: 'small firms operating in niches of demand unlikely ever to be touched by large capital. This will often entail a hand-to-mouth existence scraping around for a living' (Rainnie, 1989: 84).
4   New independent: 'small firms operating in ... specialised markets, but remaining open to the potentially fatal attractions of large firms' (Rainnie, 1989: 85).

Placing the emphasis on the external environment in which small firms may find themselves operating, Rainnie highlights how traditional ideas of independence and owner-manager prerogative in these businesses may be constrained. In interpreting his empirical material from the clothing industry, Rainnie argues that:

> it is worth noting one effect of dependency and that is a pronounced diminution in the freedom of movement open to the individual owner/manager of small clothing factories. What is to be produced under what conditions and for how much are strictly laid down. Not only is management restricted in its options, but these self-same restrictions mean that little or no interference, from the workforce, could be tolerated.
> (Rainnie, 1989: 99)

Rainnie is arguing that small firms that find themselves dependent on larger organisations, or otherwise subject to their influence indirectly, have very limited scope for determining management action. Importantly, this limits the independence for owner-managers that had been emphasised by the Bolton Report and formed a key part of the small is beautiful perspective. Moreover, the constraints operating on these dependent small firms serve to limit scope for employees to contest the ways they are managed and negotiate better terms and conditions of employment (Moule, 1998). At the same time, however, Rainnie (1989) is keen to stress that this conceptual frame is not to be viewed as a rigid classification: firms may not fit neatly under a single category, nor should we assume that all firms under one label will exhibit identical employment relationships and practices.

### Task 3.2

Think about five SMEs from a range of different industries – the wider the range you can think of the better. Now, for each of those enterprises think about its relationship with other businesses, especially clients: (i) Are all the SMEs in the same position relative to other businesses and their clients? (ii) How are the firms and relations similar or different? (iii) What might this tell us about understanding SMEs and their relationship with other businesses and clients?

Rainnie focuses his analysis on particular aspects of the external environment facing many small firms and, consequently, he over-emphasises how far into their everyday employment relationships the influence of larger firms can reach (Ram, 1991) and pays limited attention to the role of other factors that are important in shaping their employment relationships (Moule, 1998). Despite noting that, in certain circumstances, managers are 'not entirely passive victims of their circumstances [they are] well aware of the pressures that are on them and will struggle and fight to expand the limited amount of freedom to manoeuvre that they possess' (Rainnie, 1989: 117), the overall tone of Rainnie's contribution is to attribute significant influence to the constraining effect of external factors for businesses that are either dependent on large firms or operating under the threat that large businesses will move into their sheltered niche. These constraints on the scope for agency by actors within the firm are taken to influence strongly, if not always determine, the everyday employment relationships and practices within firms (Moule, 1998).

A further limitation is the extent to which the classification is able to account for the wide scope of external influences that may shape a firm's employment relationships. Rainnie's analysis focused in particular on the importance of supply-chain and competitive relations among firms within particular industries, to the extent that his analysis invited further development to enhance its ability to explain the small firm experience more generally. Subsequent work has sought to build on perspectives that emphasise a role for external influences (Gilman and Edwards, 2008), while also providing greater detail around how internal firm dynamics play a central role in shaping employment relationships.

## Interactions

In response to Rainnie's work and as part of broader developments in the field (see Goss, 1991), subsequent contributions to discussions of how employment relations in SMEs are shaped have focused more on the internal dynamics of employment relationships and broadened the scope of investigation to consider the role of a wider range of external factors. Taking these contributions together, we can see how debates around the shaping of employment relationships in SMEs have developed to acknowledge the importance of how external factors interact with the everyday goings on in places of work (Ram, 1994; Wapshott and Mallett, 2013). We can describe this second perspective as 'interactions'.

This view emerged most strongly in the ethnographic work of Ram (1994) and (Holliday, 1995), where these researchers were able to unearth the day-to-day working environments of small businesses. Through these contributions, and subsequent work such as Moule's (1998) fascinating undercover study of ButtonCo that we consider below, we are able to learn how, even in firms that are dominated by clients and competitive pressures, there remains scope for employers and employees to shape their relationships within the firm. These longitudinal, ethnographic studies report the ongoing, everyday practices within small firms that can be obscured or ignored in surveys and interviews. In her interesting methodological discussion, Holliday (1995: 19–20) adds that this detailed approach to research:

> presents a moving image rather than a static 'snap-shot' view. This permits the temporal examination of processes in a longitudinal context, and a clearer picture of actions and reaction to specific events. [It] identifies best practices for small companies to follow without any notion of the practical constraints on their implementation.

These in-depth studies of what occurs inside businesses have identified the ways in which employment relationships and practices are produced by processes of both formal and informal negotiation, of give and take between managers and employees – a 'negotiation of order' (Ram, 1994: 4). Informality allows the suitability of work practices and arrangements to be tested and ad hoc adaptations and accommodations can be refined quite quickly (see Wapshott and Mallett, 2013). These negotiations allow for the different interests to be more or less accommodated, creating idiosyncratic and potentially complex arrangements.

Some scope for relationships to be worked out on a day-to-day basis is necessary for the operation of any business with employees. Clearly, no business or system can account for every eventuality or circumstance that might arise in the conduct of business and, given the situation facing many small businesses, such scope for flexibility is necessary and inevitable. Operating in, and frequently subject to, turbulent environments (Gill, 1985), small firms can require a responsive approach to business operations that shortens planning horizons for resources and business development (MacDonald *et al.*, 2007). For example, externally a client might switch to another supplier or cease trading. Alternatively, a new rival might emerge in the same market served by the enterprise. Internally, the business might be affected by a star employee leaving to work for a rival or a member of the team absent on long-term sick leave.

Under this view, the emphasis on external factors is, to some extent, counteracted through a focus on factors arising within the firm. However, and crucially, this is not an exercise in substituting internal influences for external, but rather understanding how external and internal influences interact to create the conditions for an indeterminate range of employment relationships (Harney and Dundon, 2006; Goss, 1991). In adopting this external-internal approach, we acknowledge the caution of Arrowsmith and Sisson (1999; see also Rubery, 1994; Gilman *et al.*, 2002), who suggest such an approach is too broad to capture salient features of a particular industry sector that inform firms' operating context and, with it, the scope for determining specific practices. However, the need – and scope – for give and take between employers and employees is central to understanding employment relationships in small firms. In order to make sense of these processes, we have found that the concept of *mutual adjustment* (Mintzberg, 1980; Goffee and Scase, 1995) can be particularly helpful (Wapshott and Mallett, 2013).

Mutual adjustment concerns the informal negotiation and tacit understandings (Ram, 1999) by which individuals come to coordinate their work efforts, mediating between members of the organisation who generally interact face to face (Ram and Edwards, 2003), and reflecting the close social and spatial proximity associated with small firms. Emphasising informal communication between actors, Mintzberg (1980) suggested mutual adjustment as a reflection of the control of working practices by the 'doers'. Ram (1999) argues that this negotiation takes place in the structural context of employer/employee antagonism and cooperation, drawing out the idea that despite their necessary interdependence, employer and employee interests exist in tension.

Mutual adjustment helps to counteract the emphasis on owner-manager influence and provides a useful approach to understanding the dynamics of how employment practices are structured but may gloss over some of the more contested aspects of working lives (Ram, 1999). It reflects how workers are not helpless, 'passive recipients of management control' (Ram and Edwards, 2003: 721) but may draw on various resources to 'bargain' actively with their employers. Such explorations of mutual adjustment have begun to reveal far greater complexity and ambiguity in employment relationships and working practices than permitted by traditionally polarised accounts of working life in small firms along the lines of *small is beautiful* vs. *bleak house*.

In playing out these informal, ongoing everyday negotiations (Wapshott and Mallett, 2013), a range of factors can be seen as playing a role in shaping outcomes: the attitudes of owners and managers to their role (Harney and Dundon, 2006); family and kinship ties (Ram, 1994); perceptions of opportunities and constraints (Wapshott and Mallett, 2013); and even diverse experiences of working with each other over a period of time (see Ram, 1994; Ram et al., 2001). The significance of these various factors associated with the internal workings and relationships of a business can be fully appreciated when set within the broader context of a given organisation. When this is done it is possible to see mutual adjustment less as a somewhat static outcome and more as a dynamic process (Ram et al., 2001) which is influenced by changes that affect the business in its external and its internal environment. In other words, employment relationships are understood as dynamic and, to varying degrees, subject to ongoing, everyday negotiations (Goss, 1991).

In a clear case, employees who are held to be central to business success can use this position to negotiate better terms for themselves. Reporting on the importance of highly skilled chefs at SajCo, a restaurant trading on the quality of its distinctive food, Ram et al. (2001) present an account from the business owner complaining that he must give his chefs a pay rise when they request one. Having said this, and reflecting the dynamic nature of the employment relationship, this was also a cue for the business owner to start looking around for alternative chefs so that replacements could be employed if required, reducing the owner's vulnerability to the demands of current staff. In this way, the value of the chefs was in enabling SajCo to position itself in a competitive product market and the chefs could leverage this internally to request better pay. However, the owner was not entirely reactive in this ongoing negotiation as he sought alternative employees to alter his negotiating position.

Reporting on his time researching covertly as an employee at ButtonCo, Moule (1998) describes how unofficial smoking breaks were common on the shop floor, both in the despatch department and in the dyehouse, at the heart of the business. Although the practice was prohibited and culprits were likely to attract rebuke from the company directors, Moule observes with interest that 'proprietoral tolerance' (ibid.: 647) appeared greater for workers from the dyehouse. Explaining this observation, Moule suggests that this subtle difference in treatment of staff reflected the relative importance of dyehouse workers and despatch staff at ButtonCo. With dyehouse workers playing a more important role in meeting client demands for volume, quality and delivery time of ButtonCo's products, they had some scope for rule bending as part of the employment relationships and practices prevailing in that part of the business (see Goss, 1991). In this way, the internal and external influences interact to produce complex, negotiated outcomes.

Through these in-depth, detailed studies we can see how relationships in workplaces are influenced by numerous considerations. While degrees of interdependence exist between owners who need employees to execute tasks and employees who need employers, the balance may, at different times, favour managers or employees to some extent, often in relation to powerful external influences. If alternative labour is freely available in the external labour market and easily set to work then employers might be tempted to drive a harder bargain, believing that their current employees will not risk being replaced. Similarly, employees with skills that are in demand outside the firm, or at that particular time for their employer, might seek to exert greater influence. These ongoing, everyday negotiations are dynamic and we cannot assume that market conditions determine relations – for example, Moule details how directors in ButtonCo were careful not to overplay their hand with the despatch workers, despite their relatively weak bargaining position given their low-skilled task, because they did not want to create high levels of staff turnover.

## Multi-dimensional approach to SME heterogeneity

An appreciation of the interactions approach highlights the complexities of negotiated employment relationships in SMEs. Understanding employment relationships as negotiated, in relation to the context facing a business and actors within it, also cautions us against over-stating the role of external factors. However, one risk of arguing for the importance of context-based understandings of how employment relationships operate in small firms is that analysis becomes almost firm-specific, and it is hard to step back and build some general overviews that might provide more general understanding, business guidance or policy insights. As Ram (1994) describes, the employment relationships he observed in manufacturing SMEs were products of ongoing negotiation between employers and employees rather than domination by one or other party. Ram concluded that:

> It was not simply a question of matching work available to skill. Rather, the process was mediated by considerations like the product market, the labour market, caste and culture.
>
> (Ram, 1994: 98)

In attempting to understand employment relationships and managing people within SMEs it is therefore important to have an understanding of these different factors, which may have greater importance in some firms and less relevance for others.

To accommodate this complexity, Gilman and Edwards (2008) present a guiding framework that integrates factors we could associate with both external and internal influences on SME employment relationships and practices (see also Harney and Dundon, 2006). Organising seven dimensions (see Table 3.1) as dichotomies, the authors offer some scope for considering heterogeneity when mapping the factors that can influence employment relationships in SMEs. Not all of the dimensions will necessarily be highly salient for any given firm at a particular time, but in considering whether a firm is, for example, particularly influenced by competitive labour markets, we can attend to their specific contexts and challenges. The framework is, in this way, part of an ongoing exercise to analyse SMEs as embedded in their broader contexts (see, for example, Edwards et al., 2006). We have presented an adapted, and somewhat simplified, version of Gilman and Edwards's (2008) seven dimensions because its structure will aid our consideration of different influences acting on

Table 3.1 Influences on employment relationships and practices

| Dimension | Influence |
|---|---|
| Product market | The extent of influence from markets and competition, for example in relation to the products and services created, including the influence of clients, rivals and industry norms |
| Labour market | The degree to which pools of suitably qualified labour are available which can be accessed readily by the firm and on terms that are more or less acceptable to employer and employees |
| Resources | The extent to which the firm has ability to access resources deemed necessary to achieve its goals, such as employee skills, useful contacts and sufficient funding |
| Strategic choice | The degree to which the business has scope to pursue its preferred strategy when operating within its particular context, including perceived impacts affecting, for example, investment decisions |
| Rules and routines | The degree to which a firm's practices are formal (e.g. laid out in written policies that are implemented) or informal (ad hoc and improvised) |
| Management style | The extent to which an owner-manager seeks to exert their prerogative or involves employees in a more participatory, democratic approach |
| Networks | How widely available are collaborative, advisory and support resources to help identify and adapt to particular challenges or opportunities, how these are accessed (if at all), and to what end |

Source: Adapted from Gilman and Edwards, 2008.

SME practices as we progress through the book. However, we encourage you to study the 2006 article and the subsequent development of the framework in the 2008 paper to further your understanding and gain an appreciation of how academic ideas develop.

Gilman and Edwards (2008: 536) are keen to highlight that in presenting this framework, it 'should be used as an analytical tool and not for empirical classification'. This means that it serves to guide empirical research that raises questions of what factors, and combinations of factors (e.g. interactions between product markets and labour markets; see Ram and Edwards, 2003), shape relations in different kinds of firm rather than as an end point for classifying firms in rigid categories. The framework is also dynamic – firms can move between 'types' – for example, as they grow firms may become more formal, changing rules and routines or management style (Mallett and Wapshott, 2014; Wapshott et al., 2014).

Importantly, Gilman and Edwards build on earlier approaches (Rainnie, 1989; Goss, 1991; Edwards and Ram, 2006), grounding their framework in the established research literature we have described above. Their testing of the framework in relation to empirical materials gathered from four comparable high-tech firms reinforces the point that it is a helpful starting point to further investigation of the subtleties shaping employment relationships, while also providing sufficient structure to allow meaningful comparison of how the context of different firms can shape their employment relationships.

If we follow the analysis presented by Gilman and Edwards, among others, we should recognise clearly the potential for diversity among firms under the SMEs umbrella. Organisations that may share characteristics such as size can face very different situations owing to their wider contexts. In view of this, we should be wary of models or prescriptions of particular ways to manage in SMEs that do not attend to the different potential influences that businesses may encounter.

## Conclusion

In this chapter we have sought to set SMEs in context and have moved beyond characterisations of employment relationships and practices in SMEs as being simply either positive or negative (small is beautiful vs. bleak house). Instead we have explained how a range of factors, external and internal to a firm, interact in constructing different employment relationships and practices. The value of a context-sensitive approach is that it gets us thinking about the challenges facing firms and the limitations to owner-manager independence and ability to exert their prerogative. However, at the same time, we cannot afford just to sit deep in the detail; we must also try to step back from the specific context of each firm and understand the things that matter, perhaps in a particular industry, market and so on, and the implications this might have for similar firms.

We have presented the work of Gilman and Edwards as a means of understanding the context in which firms operate so that degrees of similarity and difference can be recognised and taken into account when comparing firms. The approach enables similar firms to be compared while not ignoring the potential ways in which these firms might differ. This tension, of grouping firms on the basis of apparent similarity while not simply smoothing over difference, carries echoes of the debate between Torrès and Julien (2005) and Curran (2006) that we raised in Chapter 1. It is inherent in the study of employment relationships and practices in SMEs, and throughout this book we endeavour to remain cognisant of it as we conduct our exploration.

# Part II
# Managing human resources

# 4 Recruitment and selection

> Recruiting and staffing is perhaps the HR topic most widely examined in the context of new ventures ...
>
> (Cardon and Stevens, 2004: 299)

In this chapter we focus on the recruitment and selection practices that may be found in SMEs, giving a variety of examples of everyday practices from the research literature and businesses with which we have worked. These examples draw out several key observations relating to how SMEs approach the matter of trying to ensure they have the right skills and capacity to achieve their objectives. The chapter will also introduce the idea of the 'deficit model', which describes the ways in which certain practices in SMEs are discussed and researched, illustrating its particular relevance to recruitment and selection.

### Task 4.1

Recruitment and selection of staff in SMEs often takes place through networks and informal contacts. We will explore this theme in the chapter, but before we do, we want you to map out your network. To do this, start with yourself at the centre of the page and map out your connections, starting with your closest connections and then spreading out on the page so that those people you know least well, but you still consider to form your network, appear at the edges of the page. Leave this to one side but keep it handy for some exercises later in the chapter.

## Why SMEs recruit and select staff

Recruitment and selection of additional staff is one response available to organisations that find current resources falling short of the demands placed upon them. The need might arise through actual or anticipated growth, skills availability, replacing staff who have left or are absent or through other factors that give rise to this mismatch between an organisation's current capacity and its operating requirements. An organisation might also face pressure to appoint new staff for less strictly operational reasons.

Tanova and Nadiri (2005), for example, report that in Turkey, many small firms employ members of the owner's family through a sense of social obligation, overcoming more operational business needs. Moreover, reflecting the types of external influence we discussed in the previous chapter, explicit or implicit demands from clients might prompt an organisation to hire more people. For instance, a client might insist on having a dedicated staff member to run their account or perhaps the owner of a client business has a family member seeking employment in the industry of their supplier. Finally, we cannot discount the personal motives of business owners, whether these be relatively philanthropic such as providing employment opportunities or driven by more personal desires for 'empire building'! In this chapter we will focus most of our attention on the functional side of bringing additional staff into an organisation.

## Practices in use

Smaller organisations tend to adopt informal approaches to recruiting and selecting staff (Forth et al., 2006). The particular techniques deployed can vary from firm to firm and depend on the type of employee required and the broader business context, but it is somewhat unusual to see the kinds of formal, multi-stage processes, involving selection tests and so on, that might be found in large organisations. However, taking a relatively informal route towards the recruitment and selection of new employees does not necessarily mean that SMEs are ineffective in their activities. In considering the range of different forms recruitment and selection can take in SMEs (see Table 4.1) and the examples we discuss below, it is important to consider how far the approaches used might serve their purpose for the businesses in question.

Table 4.1 Sources of potential employees

| Source of potential employees | Reference |
| --- | --- |
| Taking advantage of competitors or other firms making redundancies | Holliday, 1995; Marchington et al., 2003 |
| Utilising networks of contacts | Leung et al., 2006 |
| Staff recommendations | Carroll et al., 1999 |
| Employment agencies | Carroll et al., 1999; Holliday (1995) |
| Advertising vacancies | Heneman and Berkley, 1999 |
| Reappointing former employees | Marchington et al., 2003 |
| Using temporary staff to facilitate a 'try before you buy' arrangement | Doherty and Norton (2014) |
| Reviewing existing applications | Heneman and Berkley, 1999 |
| Word of mouth | Cassell et al., 2002 |

## External influences shaping recruitment and selection practices

As with other areas of managing a small firm, approaches to recruitment and selection might reflect responses to external client or industry pressures, and these external influences and constraints will shape the practices in use. During a research interview at a small business, a founder and director explained how clients contracting work for particular short-term projects, rather than engaging an agency for regular work over a period of time, led to changes in how the business considered staff appointments:

> we're looking more, it's very difficult to say ... we're looking more at project-by-project recruitment if you like, more freelance work, simply because we know that, particularly in this sector, a client has got particular start dates and finish dates. Whereas, in [another] sector, you want to keep a client and you want to hang on to them as long as you possibly can. Whereas [in this sector] clients are inclined to say, 'well, we're running a campaign from August to September', and so you need to be able to resource that at the time.

In a separate interview, his fellow founder and director continued this focus on the types of challenge faced in this industry:

> As a business we tend to find that we face time factors, for example winning a contract today [Friday] that starts on Monday. You may not necessarily have the resources in the business to do that. If the business had the luxury of two-to-three months to find the right person then I think we would find a better quality of candidate and generally that has been the experience; where we've looked for candidates in short time we haven't always ended up with the best people.

External influences on recruitment and selection can include the structure of an industry or client-supplier dynamics, and also other factors that may not be immediately apparent but have important implications for the practices adopted by firms. Martin *et al.* (2006: 394), for example, reveal how perceptions of the tourism industry in Scotland create difficulties for businesses, the majority of which are SMEs:

> the biggest challenge to the tourism employment is still the low image and low perceived status of the industry and its lack of professional career potentials and development opportunities.

In this way, external factors outside the firm's control present difficult challenges. Martin *et al.* (2006) identify that the general reputation of the tourism industry could be contributing to problems such as shortages of talented staff. Such shortages can, over time, impact on the viability of businesses but also on their ability to grow – an important issue in a sector that constitutes a significant feature of Scotland's economy. SMEs can therefore face challenging external environments in which to recruit talented staff, while having little direct influence to change these environments. For example, one small firm would find it difficult to alter the reputation of the tourism industry in Scotland. How SMEs respond to these challenges is both important and complex.

### Finding the right employee

SMEs, especially those with limited resources and facing tough challenges, need to identify employees who can contribute substantially to the business from the moment they join. However, SMEs tend not to engage with the complex selection centres or detailed assessment processes we may associate with large firms. In her account of how the production process is organised in small firms, Ruth Holliday captures a fascinating insight into the practices deployed:

> A further important selection criterion is that the potential employee is already trained. At any of the case study firms, the collapse of a local company in the same industry is viewed with relish. This leaves a pool of redundant, trained people willing to work for low wages.
> (Holliday, 1995: 144)

This quotation captures not only how some businesses conduct aspects of their recruitment and selection activities, but also how these practices take place through an interaction with their wider operating context.

The use of informal practices such as re-employing former employees who had been working elsewhere can be seen as a cost effective means of maximising information about a prospective hire and thereby reducing the risks of taking on a new employee. Kitching (2006: 882) describes how SMEs are cautious in trying to hire what they hope will be the right person owing to 'the high potential cost error'. Perhaps as a result, when we spoke to the owner-manager of a recruitment firm, he explained to us how he would employ temporary staff through agencies such as Office Angels as a means of assessing potentially permanent appointments. Taking this approach incurred the additional costs of agency fees during the temporary contract and, often, a fee on appointment. However, the additional costs were seen as a necessary insurance against the risk involved in employing a stranger which could saddle the business with an unsuitable employee. A common thread in the research literature on small firms is the importance placed on 'fit' within the workplace (see Marchington et al., 2003; Timming, 2011). With relatively few employees in an organisation, employing someone who does not fit in with the existing team could prove disruptive. A design manager at UKDesign explained to us how 'fit' was assessed at her organisation:

> We try to involve as many members of the team as possible. If we're down to say two candidates we'll maybe do a tour of the office and introduce

them to people and everyone's got a view of how they come over initially. And, from my point of view, I want everybody to participate in that process because they've got to work with that person and, if I just go off and recruit someone, they're the first to turn around and say 'he's a [expletive]' you know? You want to avoid that situation!

Perhaps heightened by the relatively close social and spatial proximity of employers and employees in many small firms, these more personal issues of fit can take on great importance. A concern with fit as well as technical knowledge led a bike repair and customisation start-up to rethink its approach to hiring apprentices. The business founder explained that he had taken on two new apprentices with a view to developing their skills and qualifications while providing a cost-effective way of increasing his business capacity. Despite the effort that had gone into the recruitment and selection process, following a traditional pattern of short-listing applicants, asking carefully constructed interview questions and so on, one of the new apprentices appeared disinterested in the day-to-day job and left. After a period of reflection, the owner hit upon the idea of a novel final selection process, as he went on to explain:

Now, we [the existing team] take candidates out for a bike ride as part of the selection process. It gives us a much better opportunity to find out about the person and their technical knowledge – for example, we can discuss cycling in general, favourite rides that sort of thing ... [The business] is built on our passion for bikes and cycling and our customers share that. Having that interest is really important but we must also be able to explain technical things to people who might just love riding!

He went on to explain that, on reflection, perhaps the traditional interview process was too easy to 'fake' compared with meeting people in more relaxed surroundings over the course of several hours. What is particularly interesting about these experiences is the innovative approach to solving a problem in a way that was directly related to the business and the particular balance of attributes it required. This is a clear example of the informality often associated with small firms, lacking sophisticated policies and processes, but it is also an excellent example of an effective, bespoke solution to an organisational problem.

However, when considering how SMEs respond to challenges, often in informal and ad hoc ways, we should be careful not to create an impression that this is the only way that firms operate. In most, if not all, firms there can be scope for both informality and formality in hiring decisions. It is important to bear in mind, as noted in Chapter 1, that while we can characterise SMEs as generally more informal than larger firms (Kotey and Sheridan, 2004; Marlow et al. 2010), we are not asserting a crude SME: informal/large firm: formal division. As Ram et al. (2001: 846) emphasise, 'Informality in small firms is ... a matter of degree and not kind, and its nature may vary as much between firms of a given size as between large and small ones'. An appreciation of the relative degrees of informality in SMEs is crucial if we are to understand their practices.

Debrah and Mmieh's (2009) paper, 'Employment relations in small- and medium-sized enterprises: insights from Ghana', provides an account of recruitment and selection at Tadi Mart which illustrates this point well. A general manager appointed from a rival firm sought to poach his former colleagues with relevant skills to advance the development of Tadi Mart. At the same time, however, these informal invitations to apply and recommendations for employment were complemented by more formal processes such as undergoing a panel interview. The Tadi Mart example, among others in the literature, highlights the importance of recognising hybrid or mixed systems where informal and formal processes may operate in tandem to achieve the ends sought by an SME as it seeks to navigate the potentially complex task of appointing new employees.

> **Task 4.2**
>
> Using Gilman and Edwards's (2008) framework, as described in Chapter 3, consider how the context in which a firm is embedded might influence its recruitment and selection practices. You might find it helpful to pick a specific firm or type of firm for this exercise and then compare your ideas with those of colleagues who have thought about a different firm or type of firm. What might this tell us about the importance of understanding the context of SMEs when considering employment relationships and practices?

## Making sense of recruitment and selection in SMEs: deficit or equivalence?

The types of study we discuss in this chapter have explored recruitment and selection activities in SMEs by attempting to understand the practices used in the operating contexts of the enterprises. The value, and necessity, of this context-sensitive approach is in enabling practices to be evaluated against the challenges they seek to overcome. Nevertheless, in the academic literature on staff recruitment and aspects of employment relationships and practices more generally, there remains a tendency to evaluate SMEs against an idealised vision of large firms.

### *The deficit model*

It is a feature of many discussions of recruitment and selection practices, and employment relationships and practices in SMEs more generally, that they are viewed through a 'deficit model' (Behrends, 2007: 57). Behrends, writing about recruitment and selection practices in professional services SMEs, describes the deficit model as arising when understandings and evaluations of HR activities are 'underpinned by a notion that regards the highly differentiated HRM-systems of large corporations as *the one best way* and therefore desirable for SMEs as well' (ibid.: 57). Models of practice that depart from this formal ideal are therefore interpreted as lacking or deficient.

The deficit model of understanding recruitment and selection activities in SMEs can predominantly be found in the research literature in two ways. The first case occurs when a typically large firm ideal 'template' is placed onto the practices of an SME and differences are found. Jameson (2000: 46), for instance, associates informal approaches to recruitment and selection with 'the informal, unsophisticated approach to the management of human resources in small firms which is characterised by vague hiring standards and unsystematic recruitment'. More recently, Doherty and Norton (2014: 138), despite acknowledging the dangers of the deficit model, go on to detail how introducing a range of more formal recruitment and selection activities in a medium-sized firm 'shows significant development of good HR practice'. There is an underlying assumption here that more formal, systematic HRM practices are superior means of recruitment and selection, and that those firms not replicating these processes are deficient in precisely those ways in which they fall short of this formal, typically large-firm, model.

The second way that the deficit model seems to be incorporated into the research literature occurs in a more implicit view that owner-managers would adopt more formal practices if only they could. Timming (2011: 572), in an interesting study that we return to below, draws on a broad range of literature to show how 'the informality of HR practices generally, and of staffing practices specifically, in SMEs' are explained. The explanations offered for the informality of recruitment and selection practices are all presented as resulting from deficiencies or lack, so 'time and resource pressures', 'knowledge-based obstacles', 'no specialist HR department' and 'little or no specialist training in personnel' are presented. In this way, SME practices are again seen as deficient and, inherently, it appears to be suggested that these obstacles must be overcome and the large-firm model embraced.

In both manifestations of the deficit model, comparisons are made with the practices of large firms' HR departments, and 'there is an implicit assumption that formal policies must prevail' (Harney and Dundon, 2007: 111). While this not only simplifies the practices of large firms, it suggests that small firms should emulate the formal practices in large firms in order to perform tasks such as recruitment and selection most effectively (Verreynne *et al.*, 2013; Greer *et al.*, 2015). Owner-managers of small firms would therefore be encouraged to adopt the policies and practices set out in a standard HRM textbook because this would ensure the effective, unproblematic management of their firm (and there would therefore be no need for this book!). In reality, a small firm may recruit very effectively using informal approaches or hybrid techniques that combine formal and informal elements, focusing on what works for their particular business (Heneman and Berkley, 1999; Verreynne *et al.*, 2013). Importing complex and, to some entrepreneurs, bureaucratic HRM models from large multinational corporations will not necessarily improve upon the effectiveness of practices in a small, locally focused business.

The deficit model of understanding practices in small firms also creates a problem in understanding recruitment and selection practices because it distracts our attention. Rather than focusing on questions of whether practices are achieving their objectives within a given context, the question is subtly reframed under the deficit model to become one of how far SME practices resemble an idealised image of practices derived from a (no doubt sanitised, formally rational and generic) representation of what is claimed to be happening in larger organisations. Given the heterogeneity of small firms as well as the changing business environments, national and local contexts and other influences and challenges, there is no single *best way* to conduct activities such as recruitment and selection.

### The equivalence model

In an attempt to combat this deficit model, Behrends (2007) argues for an *equivalence model*. The equivalence model starts from a position that organisations need to complete certain functions, such as take on new employees, but that assessing the appropriateness of particular practices for a firm should be conducted 'against the backdrop of its specific context and *action requirements*' (ibid.: 57, emphasis in original). Thinking back to Chapter 3 and our earlier analysis of practices utilising Gilman and Edwards's work, this equivalence model of understanding recruitment and selection practices underlines the importance of appreciating practices in the context of the organisation internally *and* their relation to the wider, external environment.

A detailed example of research that takes this equivalence model perspective seriously can be found in the work of Marchington et al. (2003; see also Carroll et al., 1999). Here the authors focus on the staffing practices of SMEs in the British road haulage industry where businesses were struggling to cope with labour scarcity. The businesses, most of which are small and family owned, required reliable and trustworthy employees who could work with high degrees of autonomy, transporting valuable loads to clients, to whom they would also represent the business. Perhaps echoing some of the problems identified above by Martin et al. (2006) in the Scottish tourism industry, however, the image and demands of the occupation limited the availability of good employees. Early starts and pressures for timely deliveries in spite of traffic jams were among the factors discussed by Marchington et al. (2003) as discouraging entry to the industry.

Informed by organisation objectives, labour market considerations, the nature of the work and the skills required, Marchington and colleagues analysed the recruitment and selection practices on their own terms and in the environment with which they were intended to cope. Through its rigorous investigation of the firms in the industry, this study highlights the importance placed on finding 'competent, reliable and trustworthy' drivers (Marchington et al., 2003: 14).

Such characteristics may be hard to assess formally, so we come to understand the informal practices deployed – practices such as word of mouth, a person's reputation from first-hand experience or via trusted others, re-employing former staff who left on good terms, the 'drivers network' and so on. Practical tests and trials were also used to assess driving competence, and even once appointed, new drivers might be used on local deliveries before being entrusted with full duties.

Returning to the work of Timming (2011), his paper details a similar set of informal practices predominating in the world of American and British tattoo studios. In an industry associated with 'shady individuals' (ibid.: 577), recommendations from established, trusted networks were a common source of new talent. One of Timming's respondents explained how he would always consult with the 'old men' of the industry when seeking new staff, tapping into the knowledge and networks reflecting the respondent's belief that most applicants were 'a large pile of c**p' (ibid.: 576). The highly specific focus of studies such as this usefully identifies the heterogeneity of factors at work in identifying candidates. These were reflected in the more direct means studio owners reported for evaluating prospective employees, such as appearing clean and demonstrating knowledge of the hygiene procedures to prevent cross-contamination between customers. Judgement was also exercised in relation to criminality, especially drug use. Timming (2011: 576) reports that since some drug use among tattoo artists was 'generally expected', implicit assessments of its seriousness were applied, mostly in relation to whether it affected a candidate's work.

The informal practices and use of networks to find employees in the case of tattoo artists were consistent with how the artists themselves went looking for work opportunities. Those studio owners who had used more formal means of attracting and assessing applicants reported difficulties in attracting the applicants they needed. We will return to the role of applicants and employees later in this chapter, but Timming's findings suggest how, in some sectors, prospective employees might also use their informal networks to obtain employment opportunities and evaluate prospective employers rather than have recourse to more formal processes of securing employment.

Our discussion of recruitment and selection practices has, so far, sought to highlight that relatively informal practices *can* prove effective and appropriate in meeting the needs of SMEs and the context facing the organisations. Now we turn our attention to consider some potential limitations with these approaches.

## Limitations of informal practices

While it is important not to fall into the traps of the deficit model and, instead, to evaluate SME practices on their own terms, this evaluation must also acknowledge the potential limitations of more informal approaches to recruitment and selection. As we have outlined, informal approaches, often facilitated through social ties and networks, can offer many advantages for an organisation, such as a cost-effective means of reducing the uncertainties around new staff.

58  Recruitment and selection

The limitations, and whether they represent problems, will vary from case to case depending on the circumstances of the organisation. Our aim here is to discuss the sorts of issues that can arise for an organisation conducting its recruitment and selection activities via predominantly informal means. We will focus this discussion on issues relating to finite networks, skills shortages and legislative compliance.

## Finite networks

At an operational level, networks are necessarily finite and can be exhausted. The effective 'using up' of resources available through contacts, referrals and so on could occur for various reasons. If an owner's network is not particularly wide or appropriate for their line of business, or if growth is outstripping the network's capacity to supply suitable staff, problems can arise and a change of approach may be required.

Kotey and Slade (2005) suggest that employment practices in SMEs tend to become more formal as organisations increase in size. With a particular focus on recruitment and selection activities, Kotey and Slade (2005) argue that, having exhausted informal sources of potential employees in their initial stages of growth, growing businesses resort to more formal means such as newspaper adverts and government employment agencies. These attempts to cast their recruitment net wider and attract sufficient suitable applicants can also prompt changes in how future employees are chosen from the applicants. Recruiting people from outside the family, friends and referrals network is also associated with increased use of formal processes in staff selection according to Kotey and Slade (2005). Using selection techniques, work history checks and reviewing qualifications more carefully can be understood as attempting to reduce the risks of recruiting 'strangers' into the business.

Understood in this light, we can see how informal practices, such as a reliance on personal networks, may suit businesses in some situations but can become limiting factors as the organisation, and its interaction with its environment, changes. This relates to our discussion of the Icarus paradox in Chapter 2, where changing circumstances may mean that the tried and tested approaches of the past become poorly suited to present needs or challenges. This is where evaluating the needs and challenges of individual SMEs on their own terms can be particularly important, and it can be seen that the terms of this evaluation are dynamic and subject to change owing to internal and external changes.

## Skills 'shortages'

Informal approaches to recruitment and selection via the established networks of owners and current employees may also be limited in terms of their scope. This can be clearly seen in terms of the range of skills such limited networks may struggle to provide. The literature refers to specific challenges around competence and, for example, the cultural awareness that is of relevance to organisations wishing to internationalise. In their study of SMEs in Italy, D'Angelo et al. (2013: 84) detail how family ownership and dominance of SMEs creates a 'selection bias' towards family connections. D'Angelo and his colleagues focus on the export performance of these firms and identify that the appointment of external managers promotes international export performance. Their findings suggest that breaking out of the established networks in this way can grant the firm access not only to candidates with relevant knowledge and experience of international exports, but also fresh networks of contacts who may assist in the processes of exporting internationally and entering new markets.

While avoiding the narrow determinism that Kitching (2006) cautions against, to imagine informal networks as being entirely homogenous and inward facing, it is conceivable that our informal networks might be largely constituted of people similar to ourselves in many ways. These similarities may extend to the skills or knowledge available. Over-reliance on these established networks might be suitable for some kinds of organisation and at certain times, but research such as that conducted by D'Angelo et al. (2013) suggests that there can be benefits to going beyond the boundaries of these networks. Mohr and Shoobridge (2011), for example, discuss how an ethnically diverse workforce can be beneficial for businesses interacting with diverse international markets. Benefits may accrue from employees' knowledge of international market opportunities for selling or sourcing, and this cultural know-how can reduce psychological distance between trading parties whilst also helping to reach consumers with international heritage in an organisation's home market.

## *Legislative compliance*

The question of the extent to which employment legislation and regulation impact SMEs is something to which we devote full attention in Chapter 7, but it is important to acknowledge its specific relevance to recruitment and selection practices. In an attempt to ensure fairness, the UK has legislation in place outlining the sorts of wording that should not appear in job adverts and the questions that cannot be asked in a selection interview – for example, whether or not an applicant plans to have children. A potential issue with informal approaches to recruitment and selection is that it can be hard to achieve consistent and fair treatment of all applicants. Rather than repeat here the lists and guidance available online via the UK government website, we suggest that you have a look at www.gov.uk/employer-preventing-discrimination/recruitment, or equivalent information for other countries, to provide a flavour of the issues under consideration.

Looking at economies around the world, researchers have reported interesting interactions between SMEs and regulation around recruitment decisions. In 'Selective informality: the self-limiting growth choices of small businesses in South Africa', Bischoff and Wood (2013) detail accounts of SME owner-managers avoiding additional staff recruitment in order to remain small and keep below the radar of regulators. The 'small' threshold was somewhat notional and vague but it seems to have informed business decisions. Enterprise growth was still possible, for example in financial terms, because business owners utilised outsourcing arrangements to meet demand. However, taking on permanent employees was seen as risking the greater scrutiny of regulatory compliance that would accompany firm growth beyond a particular size.

Similarly, Perraudin *et al.* (2013) explain how a clear threshold for employment rights in France shapes outsourcing decisions. They explain:

> French labour law provisions that firms may seek to circumvent by outsourcing, particularly those applying only to firms with over 50 employees, such as the requirement to set up a health and safety committee, a works council and a profit-sharing scheme, the need to establish a job protection plan if at least nine employees are made redundant in any 30-day period, and provisions on the appointment of trade union representatives.
>
> (Perraudin *et al.*, 2013: 535)

Analysing their findings leads Perraudin *et al.* (2013) to conclude that firms in France remain deliberately small in terms of employees to avoid additional regulation, but manage this through increased outsourcing (see also *The Economist*, 2014). In this way, the apparent advantages for small firms in (formal or informal) exemptions from laws and regulations can actually inhibit forms of enterprise growth. This provides a powerful example of the ways in which legislation and regulations can have important, indirect effects on SME practices (Atkinson *et al.*, 2014), and this is a theme to which we will return in Chapter 7.

While we have focused on finite networks, skills shortages and issues of compliance, there will, of course, be other potential limitations of applying informal approaches to recruitment and selection. For example, while hiring staff in terms of their interpersonal compatibility may make sense in the short term, personal relationships change over time and an employee hired for their fit with the owner-manager or the firm's culture may, in the long term, become less well-suited to the job or the business (Carroll *et al.*, 1999). Ultimately, SME practices are best evaluated according to the particular needs of the firm, the challenges it faces and its operating environment.

### Task 4.3

So far, our discussion of informal approaches to recruitment and selection in SMEs has focused on the employers' perspective: what they do to fulfil their needs in the labour market. Evaluating these practices fully, however, depends on whose perspective we adopt. While from an employer's perspective these informal approaches, often utilising established networks of contacts, can prove useful and cost effective, how might our evaluation of these practices change if we adopt the perspective of a prospective employee?

> 1   Look at your own network, mapped in Task 4.1. How diverse is it in terms of age, nationality, cultural background, experience and skills or qualifications?
> 2   Take your network map and see who could either give you a job or go a long way to helping you get a job.
>
> In this informal environment, based on contacts and referrals, you can start to see how people without regular access to business owners could struggle to gain employment in certain parts of the economy. To understand how a weak network might affect your chances of employment in this informal approach to recruitment and selection, strike out the three people most valuable or closest to you in your network and repeat task 2, above.

## Alternatives to recruitment

SMEs may be prompted by a range of factors to take on additional staff, but new hires represent just one among several potential options for increasing organisational capacity. The availability, or necessity, of alternatives can be influenced by an organisation's wider context, such as the regulatory requirements discussed above or more general social attitudes towards SMEs as attractive employers.

For many small firms, it is worth considering whether alternatives to adding headcount might be feasible. We know, for example, that some organisations deliberately forego growth that requires new staff in order to maintain a manageable enterprise that fulfils its owner's goals. Often labelled 'lifestyle' businesses, these enterprises have no intention of growing, or growing beyond a particular point (Cliff, 1998; Fletcher, 2010). In other scenarios, redesigning how work is performed, greater use of technology, prioritising certain areas of business or perhaps outsourcing certain tasks or at particular times could all represent ways of coping with problems in meeting client or customer demand. Moreover, training, which we will discuss in the next chapter, might represent an opportunity to increase the skills of current employees and help meet organisational needs. The key point to bear in mind is that taking on additional staff is just one possible response to a mismatch between an organisation's capacity and the demands it faces.

The availability of such alternatives is likely to vary between organisations depending upon their wider operating environment, both internally and externally. In their interesting overview of recruitment in SMEs, Carroll *et al.* (1999) identified that while firms of solicitors could cope with staff turnover through re-allocating work and thereby avoid fresh recruitment activity, such a response was unavailable to nursing homes. Nursing homes had to maintain *staff to resident* ratios in order to comply with the requirements of quality inspection bodies. In this context, staff turnover had to be addressed quickly through appointing new employees so that the businesses remained compliant with the regulations.

On the other hand, alternatives to appointing new staff might be deemed necessary where smaller organisations struggle in the open labour market. Presenting an image of small, family-owned businesses in Singapore, Kopina (2005) echoes the findings of Kondo (1990) in Japan and Park et al. (2014) in Korea, reporting that SMEs may be considered less attractive employers than large state-owned or multinational organisations. Kopina (2005: 486) argues that after years of negative government messages around 'archaic, unprofessional and essentially nonmodern' small firms, Singapore's highly qualified workforce tends to avoid such enterprises. Such challenges may require SMEs to seek alternatives to hiring staff.

## Conclusion

This chapter has presented a range of examples and discussion points that have sought to highlight the recruitment and selection practices used in SMEs. We have characterised these practices as predominantly, but not exclusively, informal and we have emphasised the need to understand firms as embedded in their wider contexts. From this perspective you should have started to understand how recruitment and selection can be driven by a range of factors, not all of them associated with operational need, and that these factors can change as circumstances alter. As part of this perspective, it is important to appreciate that hiring additional staff is just one potential response to capacity problems an SME might encounter.

We have identified that SMEs might use different approaches to recruitment and selection from the practices described in mainstream HRM textbooks. A key point in respect of this observation is not to fall into the trap of the deficit model. It is important to understand SME practices on their own terms and not simply as worse (or, for that matter, better) in any general sense than idealised models associated with large businesses or set out in traditional textbooks. At the same time, it is important to remember that just because the automatic assumptions contained in the deficit model can, and should, be criticised, everything SMEs do in respect of recruitment and selection is not problem free. Towards the end of the chapter we reflected on some limitations associated with the informal ways that SMEs might go about their recruitment and selection activities, and we sought to relate this to your own chances of finding a job through the network exercise. The key here is to adopt a critical and questioning approach to the practices of SMEs. We have used the area of recruitment and selection to explore the deficit model and highlight this questioning approach, but as you continue through the book and your wider reading on employment relationships and practices in SMEs, you should look out for other examples of the deficit model in use.

# 5 Training and development

In Chapter 4 we demonstrated the need to examine SMEs on their own terms, avoiding the deficit perspective from which employment relationships and practices are evaluated against an implicitly large-firm ideal. As you will have noticed already, one of the key differences between many SMEs and their larger counterparts is their relatively high degree of informality. This becomes clear when we consider training and development practices. In this chapter we seek to characterise what training and development practices in SMEs look like, we discuss why these practices are adopted, and why formal interpretations of training and development may be too narrow to build an understanding of these activities.

## Do SMEs engage in training and development?

The general picture painted in research is that smaller organisations provide less training than their larger counterparts (Hoque and Bacon, 2006). However, some have stressed (for example, Kitching and Blackburn, 2002; Kitching, 2007) that research and policy have focused unduly on formal training activities, which may not capture the predominantly informal nature of training in smaller organisations (Abbott, 1993; Jameson, 2000; Forth *et al.*, 2006). In this way, there is a risk of falling into the deficit model trap and failing to consider how informal approaches may or may not be effective for the firms that adopt them.

Reviewing the literature in relation to smaller firm training activities there are certainly a number of studies that focus on formal training and development activities, either implicitly (Huang, 2001; Matlay, 2002) or explicitly (Storey and Westhead, 1997; Westhead, 1998; Devins and Johnson, 2003). In relation to formal training, it appears that small firms do indeed provide less training than larger organisations and a number of possible reasons have been offered as to why this might be the case. Although information on engagement with formal training schemes is readily available to researchers (Westhead, 1998), studies based on these data might emphasise what smaller firms do *not* do (implicitly comparing them with larger firms or prescriptive HRM literature), rather than focusing on what training they do undertake (Massey, 2004).

A difficulty with adopting a predominantly formal model when studying training and development, as may suit traditional HRM models, is that it risks removing these businesses from the broader context in which smaller firm employment relationships are conducted (Hendry *et al.*, 1991; Goss and Jones, 1992; Kitching, 2007). As Abbott (1993: 85) contends, the limited participation of small firms in formal training 'does not mean that training in small firms is either absent or low [but rather, they] have developed their own approaches to training'.

Many SMEs face the challenges of resource poverty and their risk of mortality is especially high for the first few years of trading. Decisions of where resources are to be invested can therefore be understood in terms of whether the investment will provide a return for the business, often within a short timeframe. This is a point highlighted by Kitching and Blackburn in their 2002 report for the British government's Department for Education and Skills. Through a careful analysis of small businesses employing between two and 49 people, Kitching and Blackburn identify that among the businesses in their study:

> The incidence of training provision is associated with businesses which are larger, are in 'business and professional' and 'other' services. The composition of the labour force was also important. Those employers with workforces comprising higher proportions of professional and technical workers were most likely to provide some training in the previous 12 months. Those providing training were also more likely to report changes in the workplace in the past year, either as a result of new products and services and/or organisational changes.
> 
> (Kitching and Blackburn, 2002: x)

We recommend reading the original source document to appreciate the details of the study and the discussion, but for current purposes we can highlight a few key points. Drawing on their analysis, Kitching and Blackburn (2002: 43) devised a typology of firms based on their 'overall orientation towards training'. The typology generated from the data divides firms into three categories:

1 *Strategic trainers* described those businesses with a systematic approach to training and which had allocated a budget to these activities.
2 *Tactical trainers* were those small firms that said they trained as required but had not allocated a budget to fund any training required.
3 *Low trainers* described those respondents that reported not training in recent years or that did so only as a last resort.

Among the 1,005 firms captured in the study's telephone survey, *tactical trainers* represented the largest group with 56% of the participants; *strategic trainers* were the next largest group, comprising 29% of respondents; while *low trainers* accounted for the balance of 15%. We will return to this typology later in the chapter.

Despite this mixed picture of practice, training and development of employees is quite widely considered to be a good thing for an SME, its owners and employees. Very broadly speaking, arguments in favour of training and development relate to the idea that it is an appropriate way to increase the available knowledge or skills in a business. Barrett (2008) suggests that training for owner-managers can increase their managerial capacity, making them more effective in running their business. For employees, Aragón-Sánchez et al. (2003: 975) suggest that businesses competing on the capability and knowledge of employees should invest in staff training as a means of creating 'sustainable competitive advantages' over their rivals. Elsewhere, benefits of training are cited in terms of a sense of being valued and the creation of loyalty amongst employees who benefit from investments in their personal development (Beynon et al., 2015).

We spoke to a senior designer at a small, growing design company about his experiences of training and development:

INTERVIEWEE: They're very good at funding, not just stuff that's related to [your job]. You know, if you decide to do something, they will go as far as they can to support you.
RW: And is that, say, when there's a designer and they want to become a project manager or something?
INTERVIEWEE: Well, that happened. Allison was an art worker. She's become a project manager and, to be honest with you, in terms of development, they're second to none. They'll help you do anything you want to do. I think Sandy got the FA Coaching thing paid for and Linda's life-drawing classes were paid for.

It was part of a wider theme around how employees at this firm were viewed, according to the chief executive:

I think, the work, certainly the way that we do approach management of people and certainly my approach is that I truly believe if people are happy in their what they're doing and their work they'll be good at it and we'll be able to reap the benefits of that, their expertise and creativity. In having a really successful business, so everything that we're doing and we have been doing for the last few years in terms of managing people, having teams and developing people and allowing them to do more or less what they want to do within reason, is to make sure people are happy and content and really like working at here ... I have talked to a few people about having a happy-o-meter erm, not quite sure what the indicators on the happy-o-meter are going to be, but I suppose one way to measure is whether or not the happiness factor is working is staff retention and, I have to say, we do have a very high [rate of staff] retention.

A belief in the benefits of training in smaller firms has led to policy support being targeted at this area. Devins and Johnson (2003) present findings from a study of the European Social Fund, part of the European Union's support for employment and social inclusion through a focus on skills development. Specifically, Devins and Johnson discuss one initiative in Britain, which sought to help:

> alleviate the threat of social exclusion through long-term unemployment by developing the skills of the workforce who were employed but potentially at risk of losing their jobs. However the potential to contribute to the competitiveness of SMEs through the development of improved training and development processes was also a key driver.
> (Devins and Johnson, 2003: 214)

Devins and Johnson's analyses led them to suggest that the perceived beneficial impact of training activities, undertaken through the programme, was greatest in businesses with 25–49 employees, but lower than average for micro firms and those employing more than 100 people. The authors suggest that policy should aim at promoting the economic benefits of training to this group of SMEs employing 25–49 people to encourage investment in staff training. However, the findings from this study were not entirely clear-cut (not all differences identified were statistically significant) and we should always be wary of generalisations by firm size.

The positive associations with training and development activity and business performance provided in the literature are challenged by Storey (2004: 125), who argues that 'there is, at best, only weak evidence that those small firms providing formal external workforce training perform better than those that do not'. As with recruitment and selection, this suggests that the approaches to and impacts of training and development in SMEs are far from straightforward and there are no particular effects or strategies that can be easily generalised. We will return to assessments of the costs and benefits of training for SMEs later in this chapter, but first we need to consider some of the other factors that influence the decision to engage with training and development.

## What influences training and development provision in SMEs?

To develop a more nuanced understanding of training and development in SMEs we need to set out the factors that are considered to influence its provision. In Table 5.1 we provide an overview of the key influences, together with relevant academic references that have provided insight into each area.

Our objective here is to map out the territory rather than engage in detailed discussion of the drivers of training and development identified in the literature. Clearly, there are commonalities with the more general discussion of influences that shape employment relationships in Chapter 3. The key theme that emerges is the response of smaller firms to external challenges and influences, and specifically the often informal ways in which they respond to these. For example, in his South African study, Hirschsohn (2008) distinguishes the approach of SMEs to training and development from the typically 'textbook' approach that

Table 5.1 Influences on training in SMEs

| Influence | Description | Key references |
|---|---|---|
| Pressing business need | When training offers a solution to a current and pressing problem; tactical solutions to crises | Jayawarna et al., 2007; Hirschsohn, 2008 |
| Change within the organisation | Major changes in the ways firms work, prompting the need for new skills/capabilities | Jones, 2005; Kitching and Blackburn, 2002 |
| Innovation and innovative businesses | Businesses competing on the novelty or differentiation of their product line may require staff to have the latest skills | Kitching and Blackburn, 1999; Macpherson and Jayawarna, 2007 |
| Relations with large businesses | When forming part of a large business supply chain, particular types of training might be necessary | Macpherson and Jayawarna, 2007 |
| Participation in business networks | Relationship between membership and levels of training (may not be causal) | Hoque and Bacon, 2006 |
| Business size | Provision of formal training increases rapidly as businesses experience the initial stages of growth | Kotey and Folker, 2007 |

sees training and development *integrated* with a particular business strategy. Consistent with understandings of HRM in SMEs more generally, Hirschsohn argues that considerations of staff skills receive a lower priority than questions of product market, competitive strategy and operations decisions such that considering what to do about training and development is often a response to particular business needs rather than forming part of a deliberate strategy.

Adopting Kitching and Blackburn's (2002) three-part typology of *strategic, tactical* and *low* trainers, Hirschsohn (2008) identifies through his analysis of 13 cases how competitive forces in their market segments, along with plans for business growth, strongly influence approaches to training and development. In his study, the strategic trainers 'relied on high-level professional skills for competitive success and either had ambitious growth plans or faced intense international competition and labour market shortages for critical skills' (ibid.: 200). It was important for businesses in these competitive markets to maintain skill levels because this was central to their line of work. In contrast, the tactical trainers competed in relatively mature markets, were generally not targeting significant growth and could access readily any skills requirements via the labour market. The one example of low trainers presented by Hirschsohn was a food processing business facing limited competition that might demand new ways of working to achieve production efficiencies, which in turn require staff training. Since the work involved was low skilled and tasks easily learned, the business had little incentive to train the workforce.

In some instances decisions to undertake some form of staff development, as with other areas of human resource management, may be out of owner-managers' hands. Macpherson and Jayawarna's (2007) paper, 'Training approaches in manufacturing SMEs: measuring the influence of ownership, structure and markets', sets out to consider the kinds of influence that can shape training and development approaches. A questionnaire was sent to owner-managers of SMEs engaged in engineering and manufacturing businesses. Among the interesting findings they present, Macpherson and Jayawarna highlight the importance of a firm's relationship with larger businesses. Macpherson and Jayawarna found that those businesses working mainly 'within the supply chain of a larger company, also adopt more intense and more formal approaches to training' (ibid.: 712). Although they do not discuss this finding in detail, it offers an opportunity to reflect on how larger firms might influence aspects of SMEs' employment relationships and practices (see, for example, Rainnie, 1989).

Beaumont et al. (1996), writing about businesses of various sizes, suggest how supply chain relationships can exert influence on employment relationships and practices both directly and indirectly. Direct influence describes instances when 'the customer organization may establish an auditing instrument for its suppliers which asks a series of questions about the existence (and performance) of certain employee relations practices and arrangements in the supplier organization' (ibid.: 13). For example, a client organisation might decide that it wants its suppliers to maintain Investors in People accreditation. In contrast, indirect influence is used to describe relationships in which:

> increased customer demands for improved supplier performance, increasingly supported by the results of auditing instruments, necessitate the supplier organization making internal changes to their management systems and techniques, and their working practices/arrangements in order to meet the increased expectations and demands of customers.
>
> (Beaumont et al., 1996: 13)

In this instance, the client may require cost savings directly which indirectly require their suppliers to change work practices and train their staff as a consequence of these changes. The ability of a firm to contest or resist the direct or indirect influences of its clients will depend on various factors, not least its perceived ability to negotiate with the client or survive losing its custom (see Swart and Kinnie, 2003).

### Task 5.1

Reflect on the example of training and development in SMEs that have close links with large businesses. Why might the larger business insist on certain training and development requirements being fulfilled?

What does this tell us about the independence of SMEs and the importance of understanding a firm's wider context when trying to account for employment relations and practices in these firms?

The key point here is that, as we might expect, there is a range of influences on the motives behind training and development activity. What emerges when we begin to look at these influences and their impacts are the relatively informal and ad hoc approaches that differ markedly from textbook approaches to HRM developed from larger firms. However, before considering the practices that emerge in response to the various influences, we must also consider the different constraints that act upon SMEs and their engagement with training and development.

## What constrains training and development in SMEs?

Much of the literature discussing training and development provision in SMEs focuses on those factors that limit engagement with training and development. Identifying these constraints is important in building understanding of how training and development operates in relation to SMEs. Although the literature tends to focus on 'barriers' to training and development, we would rather frame constraints on training provision as factors that shape how training and development is viewed and deployed. We will expand on this perspective in the next section when we consider the drivers and constraints together in building a picture of how training and development functions in SMEs.

There is some discussion over whether the apparently limited engagement with training and development in SMEs results from demand-side issues, meaning SMEs do not *want* training provision, or from limited supply, meaning training providers do not meet SME *needs*. Starting with explanations attributed to demand-side problems, limited management awareness of training provision available (Lange et al., 2000), as well as a limited ability to identify their training needs (Abor and Quartey, 2010) and assess training options (Vickerstaff, 1992) have been identified as influential factors. Others have cited the influence of the owner-manager's attitude towards training and development as vital to its role and provision within a firm (Matlay, 1997; Kitching and Blackburn, 1999), although Birley and Westhead (1990) have warned against assuming the dominance of particular actors.

Owner-manager attitudes are drawn out by Kitching and Blackburn (1999), who conducted a study of manufacturing SMEs in the United Kingdom (London), Germany (Stuttgart) and Denmark (Aarhus). Considering the propensity of these businesses to access external training provision, Kitching and Blackburn found that the businesses in London tended to operate on a subcontractor basis for clients who set tight specifications that could be met through established technologies. As a result, these businesses did not have an immediate pressure to acquire new skills from outside the business and training was not a priority. Kitching and Blackburn (1999: 427) quote an owner-manager as explaining:

> It's one of those things you can muddle by. With a machine tool you need to know how to run it otherwise it's not going to run. With managerial

> skills it's one of those grey areas that things will carry on running if not particularly well ... My training is really about the performance of the machine tool and not so much as to whether Joe Bloggs can cover health and safety because he's been trained for it. That's the way it goes. That's the real world. The real world is that machines have to go so that we get some money in the building. Unless we get some money in the building, the training's academic. You can have the best trained people in the world but if you've got nothing to do ...

This may also have influenced the owner-managers' attitudes to training providers. Another owner-manager stated:

> We obviously don't see a need. I think it's becoming an industry in itself and there's a lot of people earning a bloody good living out of it. From our point of view, we don't see a need for it ...
> (Kitching and Blackburn, 1999: 427)

The experience of businesses in London was contrasted with those in Stuttgart and Aarhus which were engaged in more innovative and original products, utilising newer technologies. The importance of innovation to these continental-European businesses was, among other factors, an influence on their recourse to external training provision. These owner-managers also reported being more likely to see themselves as part of a network with the training providers, based on relationships developed over many years that were seen as sustaining the businesses' competitiveness.

Considerations of cost and the likely return on investment in training are important elements in demand-side issues. Smaller businesses may face higher costs per employee for training since they cannot divide costs over significant headcounts in the way that large companies can (Lynch, 1994). The impact of having one employee off-site for training is also likely to affect smaller firms to a greater degree than it would for a business where one person is a tiny proportion of the total workforce (Lynch and Black, 1998). Such 'frictional effects' (Bryan, 2006: 639) must be borne in mind when thinking about the types of training that might be suitable for SMEs.

Because of these costs, without clear and consistent evidence that training and development boosts organisational performance, owner-managers might be reluctant to invest resources unless it responds to an immediate business need. Moreover, the fear of employee turnover may cool demand for training in SMEs that are unwilling to train staff who then leave for rival businesses (Jones et al., 2013). However, Kitching and Blackburn (2002) have argued that the fear of poaching is overstated, given that employers must often provide at least basic training to enable tasks to be completed and, further, that the firm-specific nature of training limits its portability. Perhaps a revised understanding of the 'poaching' issue could recognise that the effects of the risk may be particularly relevant to externally validated training (for example, where it leads to qualifications), which can become valuable 'currency' for employees in the labour market (Storey, 2004).

This can be illustrated with a specific example. In recent years road cycling has become popular in the UK, as it is already in many parts of continental Europe. Anyone wanting to work in the industry as a bike technician may find that they need to be Cytech qualified, an industry-created qualification based around particular skills. A quick read around cycling forums suggests that many of the skills covered through Cytech can be gained without the qualification, so it offers a good example of how qualifications might operate in the jobs market. A job applicant who possesses formal qualifications may be attractive to a prospective employer, whether stipulating Cytech qualifications in a job advert or not, because the employer knows the standards to which the candidate has been trained and the degree to which they should be able to integrate within the existing team. The perceived risk of hiring a new employee may be reduced. We could contrast this kind of externally validated competence with the sorts of training that might be acquired in-house and on the job. The technician who can fix bikes just as well as the qualified technician but has learned exclusively on the job and whose ability has not been evaluated independently might have a harder time convincing potential employers of the range and depth of their competence. So, while the unqualified technician could still find work with another employer, this might prove more difficult in some instances than if they had externally validated industry qualifications.

A focus on meeting short-term business needs and the fear of training not providing a return on investment may influence an apparent tendency for SMEs to 'buy-in' management talent and skills when it is required rather than training their own staff. This then creates a demand for employees trained elsewhere. Hirschsohn (2008) reports how, in his study, most firms hired the skills they needed as required. Such behaviour among firms might create and sustain a situation in which firms are reluctant to train, given a fear of poaching by other firms, so instead recruit staff from the external labour market (and those other firms) to meet their business needs. Further, even if training does not lead to staff turnover (see Beynon et al., 2015), SMEs could still face the challenge of how to utilise effectively the skills developed among their existing employees. Many SMEs operate with relatively flat hierarchical structures and, especially the smallest firms, may be reluctant to develop employees who will then have capacities that outgrow their current position while the business has limited scope for offering promotion (Bryan, 2006; Hoque and Bacon, 2008).

While an appreciation of potential demand-side constraints is important to understanding an apparent reluctance to train in SMEs, this must be understood next to supply-side considerations. There are important questions, for example, over whether training providers are focused on SMEs. Reporting from Nigeria, Mambula (2002) bemoaned the lack of training and information available to those seeking to start up a new business, potentially frustrating efforts to build SMEs. To overcome the reported skills shortage among owners and potential business owners, and key staff, Mambula floats the idea of an 'alliance of government, research institutions, and finance establishments to create appropriate training for prospective small businesses' (ibid.: 64). Moreover, Mambula goes further to suggest that only those managers who demonstrate competence in completing the necessary training should be eligible for loans from the development banks engaged in supporting business start-up. Using training as qualifying criteria would be intended to help tackle the risk-averse banks' reticence over lending to untrained business owners while also addressing perceptions of nepotism influencing loan decisions in the country.

A lack of SME-focused training providers may stem from perceived attitudes among owner-managers, as explained by Kitching and Blackburn (1999: 628):

> Business owners' attitudes towards training, and those of training providers, were mutually reinforcing. Anticipating a reluctance to train on the part of owner-managers, suppliers of training focused their efforts where they were most likely to generate a return, that is, on larger enterprises.

## The shape of training and development in SMEs

In the chapter so far we have sought to identify the kinds of considerations that can have a bearing on the levels and types of training provision in SMEs. In this section we reflect on these considerations to discuss how they come together to shape training and development, and also think about what we might learn about employment relations in SMEs more generally through a focus on training and development.

As we have discussed, training and development might be prompted by issues including change within a business or other kinds of immediate business need. While this might prompt a requirement for training provision, it could also be tempered by some of the perceived constraints. Owner-managers may be cautious over training investments that may not provide a return or could lead to the trained staff leaving the business, having been made more valuable in the labour market. Bearing in mind these drivers and constraints, it may be unsurprising that training and development in SMEs is typically regarded as occurring along informal lines. The responses to external influences, in tension with owner-manager prerogative and a short-term focus, can provoke ad hoc responses to the latest challenges, producing practices developed in relation to particular problems. Importantly, therefore, SME practices can be considered an ongoing attempt to balance between competing forces, as the organisation tries to match its internal and external environments (Phelps et al., 2007; Levie and Lichtenstein, 2010).

In the case of training and development, the clearest example of informal ad hoc responses to particular needs such as training new staff can be seen in terms of on-the-job training. Importantly, this is not something exclusive to smaller firms; many organisations will engage in this to some degree and it is a valuable form of interaction and an effective method of learning new skills. However, it may be more prevalent in SMEs, which typically engage in less formal, external forms of training. For example, a detailed study of SMEs and training provision by Goss and Jones (1992: 20) report an owner-manager describing their approach to training and development:

> In all honesty we don't need to give much training. All the work here is machine work and all the people doing it are experienced. When someone new comes the old hands will show them the ropes and they will pick it up from there. It's just like a family thing really, we help each other.

Some of the attractions for firms relying on informal or on-the-job training (Hendry *et al.*, 1991) include its relevance for specific tasks or the firm more generally (Lange *et al.*, 2000; Kitching, 2007). Cost and convenience of providing training in-house, as well as the clear communication of employers' performance expectations, are further reasons cited for informal training in small firms (Kitching and Blackburn, 2002). However, this shifting, ad hoc nature of training provision has caused problems for researchers and distorted the ways in which it is understood. Smith *et al.*'s (2002) review indicates that informal training is not always identified as such by those providing it during the normal course of their work, making it hard for researchers to detect. Upskilling an employee by these informal means to meet an immediate demand may not be labelled as training within the firm or even seen as anything other than the day-to-day running of the business.

This ad hoc approach creates the potential for problems due to a lack of long-term strategy. Further, despite its obvious attractions for some firms and its advantages over formal training, in-house, informal practices still require resources so carry the 'frictional effects' highlighted by Bryan (2006: 639) above. For example, on-the-job training can require an existing worker to take time out of the production cycle in order to instruct a novice (Holliday, 1995). Beyond the initial training, the new employee might require further supervision, which again could impact upon their own productivity or that of others. This suggests that while training and development in small firms may be legitimately characterised as predominantly informal, some of the same challenges may still apply.

## Investors in People: a formal approach to training for predominantly informal firms

The seeming preference for informal practices in SMEs raises questions about initiatives intended to encourage training and development in the workforce. For example, Investors in People (IiP) started out as a means of recognising businesses that invested in particular types of staff training and development (see Ram, 2000; Hoque and Bacon, 2008). The accreditation has been viewed as sufficiently successful to expand its scope to a more general 'high-performance' agenda (not to mention vague management-speak):

We optimise performance by championing best practice in people management and equipping our organisations with the tools to succeed. Organisations that demonstrate the Investors in People Standard achieve our accreditation through a rigorous and objective assessment to determine performance.

(www.investorsinpeople.co.uk/about)

Nevertheless, IiP represents a useful seam in the research literature to explore how government-backed formal initiatives might fare among SMEs. We focus here on the initial guise of IiP, focused on training and development and attracting some interesting academic work on its efficacy and value.

There are concerns that perceptions among owner-managers that the assessment for IiP status is overly bureaucratic (Hoque and Bacon, 2008) may dissuade participation – that is, unless the accreditation is required by clients, and in these instances the risk arises of IiP being obtained for external 'show' purposes rather than as a deep engagement with practices. In Ram's (2000) study of IiP-accredited SMEs, he provides evidence that the award did little to influence the day-to-day provision of training in the businesses. Instead, IiP was treated as a paper exercise that the businesses could use to promote themselves. As a senior employee in one organisation studied by Ram explained:

> Our business will run perfectly efficiently – if that is the correct word – without IiP. We want Investors in People because we want to do business with the TEC and the TEC requires that you have IiP by March '97 ... So to give an example, when I go and see the IiP person [assessor] ... Because I am a senior member of staff ... I will talk to them positively and say the right things, but deep down if I said the truth, you know, we probably wouldn't get it. Because the truth is that we have a document that doesn't relate to members of staff. It is just that people have sat down and written out a list of procedures.
>
> (Ram, 2000: 80)

We found a similar story in our own research. In one firm, obtaining IiP was influenced by a desire to appear more credible to stakeholders. A founder and director explained:

INTERVIEWEE: I know you can have IiP if you employ two people but we wanted to have these processes in place so that we would grow into them. And so we wanted to get them right early on so that we weren't ambushed by issues and problems as we started to change from, I suppose, quite a cosy little company into more of a normal business where, inevitably, some day, there's going to be friction or difficulty. And, to be fair to everybody, you need proper procedures. So why not get IiP, get it done properly? Also, I think we felt it sent a good message out about us, not just to potential employees but the fact that we were sort of a bona fide, strong business.

RW: Has that actually introduced any additional complexities into the business?
INTERVIEWEE: No, it has, it hasn't actually. It's been pretty helpful to know that, to have the procedures, the proper procedures in place. But I don't know [sigh]. What I sense is, in a way, that they [the procedures] are perhaps not as active as they should be because they, I think they kind of sit in the, they're not necessarily sat in the cupboard but, but they're not something I think about every other day. Perhaps they should be, I don't know.

## Formal policy versus informal practice

The relative formality of IiP, set in the context of typically informal SMEs, gives rise to the policy/practice distinction of which we should be aware when studying all organisations. When looking at employment relationships and practices in SMEs, it is especially important to understand that the policies in place might not be matched in the day-to-day practices of the organisation. A good example of this was provided by Bacon et al. (1996) in their paper on employment relationships and practices in SMEs.

As part of an investigation into the employment relationships and practices of organisations in Leicestershire, England, already touched on in Chapter 3, Nicolas Bacon and his colleagues present analysis of findings from a telephone survey of SMEs in a region of the UK. Contrary to finding 'bleak house' (Sisson, 1993) conditions, as may have been anticipated, results suggested high take-up of 'new management' practices such as culture change programmes, devolved management, team working and performance appraisals. The telephone survey of 'the most senior manager on site responsible for human resource management' (Bacon et al., 1996: 84) gathered responses from 229 businesses, divided into categories employing 15–24 people (95 firms) and 25–199 people (134 firms). Some 13 of the firms were then followed up with face-to-face interviews of owner-managers or directors. These follow-up interviews revealed degrees of 'over-claiming' (ibid.: 88), as illustrated by this example from one business visited:

> At the Hotel we discovered people management ranked low on the business agenda. The culture change programme was, in reality, little more than 'trying to impress on the staff the importance of giving customers what they want'. Devolved management was 'if one of the girls starts to do a bit more, then that's fine, I'll leave her to it'. Teamworking was the notion that 'we are all a team and have to muck in together'. A performance appraisal was 'I'll keep my eye on those that are not doing what they should, if someone does that bit extra and really helps us out then I'll slip them a bit more money in their pay packet'.
> (Bacon et al., 1996: 88)

The presence of over-claiming in some of the firms Bacon et al. researched is interesting in several respects. First, we should acknowledge that some owner-managers may be presenting a more formally 'sophisticated' approach to employment relationships and practices than exists in practice. As with all things, what people say they do and what they do in practice can be quite different! There were still practices similar to the 'new management' the researchers had initially set out to identify, but the firms tended to operate along less formal lines than might be understood in the context of larger organisations. In their analysis, Bacon et al. (1996) draw out an interesting observation that 'the meaning of these terms in the small business setting as our respondents understood them was quite different from how managers in larger organizations used the concepts' (ibid.: 90). In other words, they highlight the importance of understanding the practices *behind* the labels used to describe certain activities. The value of this more critical approach is that it helps us not only to avoid the problems of looking for large firm or textbook practices in small firms, but also to take the practices found in small businesses on their own terms.

Even where practices conforming to the familiar labels are present, day-to-day training and development practices may involve forms of both formality and informality. For example, when formal external training is provided, there can be informal mechanisms used to share the skills and knowledge acquired. Similar to the findings of Smallbone et al. (2000), in our research we have come across businesses that agree to fund attendance at external training for employees on the condition that the employees relay the training to colleagues when they return. In this way, the boundary between formal and informal training and development is blurred. The same might be said of employment practices in SMEs more generally – the balance of informal and formal practices, while generally in favour of the former, must always be interpreted with reference to the practices in use within a business and its operating context.

This suggests some of the complexities involved in trying to characterise people management practices in SMEs. When emphasising the informal practices of SMEs, contrasted with more formal large firms, we must be careful not to get carried away with thinking that the distinction is anything more than a convenient shorthand. The distinction is helpful in orienting us away from an assumption that we can transpose the practices of large businesses onto smaller organisations. At the same time, though, it would be an error to consider SMEs as universally informal or large firms as simply formal. Further, differences in the training provision available to different grades of worker in the business data studied by Hoque and Bacon (2008) lead them to suggest 'small' and 'medium-sized' businesses should be treated as distinct when trying to understand approaches to training and development. When studying employment relationships and practices we must pay careful attention to organisational context and the practices in use.

## Conclusion

In this chapter we have considered the place of training and development in SMEs. Through our discussion of the research literature we have suggested that the commonly cited conclusion that smaller firms are poor trainers, while perhaps holding some truth, may mask important contextual factors that distinguish firms from each other and help explain firms' particular approaches (Goss and Jones, 1992; Gibb, 1997; Patton *et al.*, 2000; Kitching, 2007). A theme that should be becoming clear by this stage in the book is the importance of trying to locate SMEs in their context when seeking to understand and evaluate aspects of their employment relationships and practices. In so far as we can ever discuss 'an' or 'the' SME context, for owner-managers it seems that they have scope to set out an approach to training and development, but this ability may be more or less constrained by a number of (at times) competing demands, objectives and opportunities. What emerges within this context tends towards a set of informal and somewhat ad hoc practices around training and development. As a result, focusing attention predominantly on formal means of training and development can limit understanding of training and development practices in SMEs.

We conclude by drawing on the work of Storey (2002: 260), who leans more towards 'smaller firm relevance' than 'large firm comparisons'. This underlines how the context and challenges facing SMEs should be accounted for in building our understanding. In light of the book so far, we feel this sentiment can be taken as a general guide for further study of employment relationships in SMEs.

# 6 Reward and recognition

Just as recruitment and selection or training and development can be necessary activities for many businesses, irrespective of their size, organisations also have to reward their workforces for the work they do. This chapter considers the issues of reward in SMEs, along with how these businesses recognise employee contributions and broader issues of performance management. The value of dealing with the topics of reward and recognition together is that it allows discussion of non-economic benefits and satisfaction, which, as we discussed in Chapter 3, have been suggested as trade-offs for the lower pay predominant in many SMEs and relate to broader debates around job satisfaction in these firms.

These discussions are located, necessarily, within the wider context of the employment relationship and we will consider why SMEs might struggle to adopt more complex, or 'sophisticated', performance management systems, as associated with models of HRM. Reward and recognition play an important role in the ongoing negotiation in firms around control and autonomy, efficiency and equity. This topic will therefore also provide a platform for discussing informal means of linking rewards and performance and the centrality of owner-manager prerogative within SMEs.

## Reward and recognition in SMEs

It is generally accepted that financial rewards are lower in SMEs than what might be found in large organisations (Arrowsmith *et al.*, 2003; Cox, 2005). Even the 1971 Bolton Committee Report, which reflected mainly management perspectives, conceded that pay in SMEs is generally less than might be found in larger organisations. The report concluded, however, that '[t]he fact that small firms offer lower earnings than large firms suggests that convenience of location, and generally the non-material satisfaction of working in them, more than outweigh any financial sacrifice involved' (Bolton, 1971: 21). That is, SMEs pay less but, Bolton suggests, employees have higher job satisfaction that compensates for this lower pay.

Consistent with the view expressed in the Bolton Committee Report, Ingham (1970) went so far as to suggest that workers in SMEs may actively choose employment in 'small, low-wage organizations with a low level of bureaucratization' (ibid.: 50), reflecting their relative preferences for non-economic rewards over economic rewards. In this sense, lower economic rewards can be, in some ways, traded-off against other perceived rewards or benefits that may be derived from working in an SME. This perspective on reward in SMEs, calculating overall 'reward' by combining economic and non-economic elements, has remained influential in studying employment relations in SMEs.

Scott and Rainnie (1982: 176), reflecting on the Bolton Report and presenting contrary empirical evidence, explain that:

> the Ingham/Bolton view of industrial relations in the small firm has over time crystallised into a sort of unchallenged conventional wisdom.
>
> This is hardly surprising given that the largely uncritical acceptance of the advantages to the economy of a viable and healthy small firm sector has translated itself, at least in terms of research, into a concentration on stimulating entrepreneurship, business survival rates, sources of finance, etc. In other words, as long as we can ensure the survival of an endangered species, the small businessman, we know that the workforce will be alright because the conventional wisdom tells us so.

More recent findings, from an analysis of the 2004 Workplace Employment Relations Survey (a national survey of British workplace employment relations; see BIS 2013), by Blackburn et al. (2007) appears to find some support for the idea that workers in smaller enterprises may be less dissatisfied than their counterparts in larger organisations. Blackburn and his colleagues are, however, reluctant to interpret these findings as necessarily highlighting an inherently satisfactory employment experience in smaller enterprises. Rather, the authors follow Forth et al. (2006) in suggesting that smaller businesses may tend to lack some of the factors that give rise to dissatisfaction in larger organisations, such as problems arising from compressed pay rates. More positively, the close social–working relationships often associated with SMEs may allow some scope for employer and employee needs and wishes to be accommodated through degrees of give and take, and we will discuss such forms of negotiation later in this chapter.

Reflecting back to the ideas we covered in Chapter 3, where we considered how various factors help to shape employment relationships and practices in SMEs, Curran and Stanworth (1981) offer a critical perspective on working life in SMEs. In their examination of smaller firms in the printing and electronics industries, Curran and Stanworth concur that, while not entirely absent from research literature at the time, 'so much of the writing on the small firm employee simply assumes a knowledge of his motivation and attitudes without any rigorous examination of these assumptions' (ibid.: 142). While it is well worth reading the original paper yourself to appreciate how they build their argument, for current purposes we can highlight how Curran and Stanworth characterise small-firm employees as being generally younger, less well-trained and more prone to job switching than their large business counterparts.

Through their analysis, Curran and Stanworth (1981: 145) argue 'that small firm workers did not so much self-select themselves into jobs as a result of possessing certain stable motivational patterns but rather developed a market situation in which their job choices were often highly circumscribed'. Reflecting similar concerns, Rainnie (1989: 170–177) provides a detailed analysis of Ingham's proposition to demonstrate how the apparently active preference for employment in small businesses, along with lower wages, might reflect less workers' self-selection and more a lack of higher-paying alternatives open to them. In light of this analysis, the sense of active preference or choice underlying Ingham's (1970) evaluation of rewards in SMEs can be questioned. These factors will become important as we develop our understanding of the reward and recognition practices in use in SMEs and, in particular, the forms of negotiation that may inform such practices.

## Practices in use

As with other accounts of employment practices of SMEs adopting a 'deficit perspective', Cardon and Stevens (2004: 307) question whether 'small firm managers take a systematic and rational approach to compensation, as traditional HR research would suggest is best'. Before we discuss this perspective in detail, we should describe the kinds of practices that are associated with reward and recognition in SMEs.

When considering only economic rewards in SMEs there can be risks in too narrow a focus on basic wages (Cox, 2005). As with any type of business, financial rewards in the form of a basic, regular wage may capture only one element of an employee's total remuneration. Scott et al. (1989), for example, distinguish between wages and take-home pay because overtime might boost the latter figure beyond the earnings of someone in a large firm. The crucial difference is that overtime is not guaranteed or necessarily regular. Others have highlighted pay systems that incorporate elements that are contingent on some element of performance. For example, studying employment practices in Australian businesses across various sectors employing between ten and 200 people, Wiesner and Innes (2010) report evidence of practices including pay based on individual performance and acquired skills, as well as collective performance schemes such as company or team performance reward arrangements. Elsewhere, Cassell et al. (2002), in a study of UK managers' views on the presence and efficacy of HRM practices in SMEs, conducted research into aspects of participant firms' selection, appraisal, reward and development practices as well as the presence of formal HR strategies. Considering the findings in relation to reward, the author's note that almost half of the businesses they surveyed reported some form of performance-related incentive scheme in its reward structures. Reporting on a study of employment practices in China's SMEs, Zheng et al. (2006) also indicate relatively high levels of reported performance-related pay practices, especially in comparison with more traditionally run state-owned enterprises.

Reports of these performance-related pay practices are interesting in the context of SMEs because of the tendency for relatively informal approaches towards other aspects of employment relationships and practices. Performance-related pay arrangements imply that there are means of tracking performance at the desired level (individual, team, business), and of setting suitable targets in terms of what employees can achieve and a business can afford. These degrees of formal complexity, the integrated measurement and assessment of performance against strategic targets, seem somewhat at odds with the typical picture of employment practices in SMEs.

However, while performance-related pay sounds very formal and sophisticated and may be reported as such in brief telephone surveys with the firm's owner-manager, such approaches to reward and recognition can also be highly informal – for example, the informal and ad hoc provision of extra cash in the pay packets of those the boss thinks are particularly hard working or loyal. Part of an explanation for how this apparent mismatch between perceptions of formality and informal practices in use arises can be found by returning in more detail to the work of Cassell *et al.* (2002).

This study followed up an initial telephone survey with in-depth interviews involving senior managers at a sample of SMEs. The study identified a large diversity of practices in use. In the case of reward and recognition, they identify that many of the firms claiming to have adopted some form of incentive pay arrangement also said that they struggled with making it work effectively. An illustrative quotation presented by the authors provides an interesting example:

> My worry is that at the moment we have these little systems we do not properly police, because to police them is an administrative nightmare. Even for a company this size with 100 people on the clock, say 70 of them are on piecework [and] you would need at least two or three full time people doing nothing but piecework timing.
>
> (Cassell *et al.*, 2002: 685)

It could be that there are SMEs with some form of performance-related pay arrangements in place but, nevertheless, struggling to make them work effectively. In such instances, ad hoc solutions to the problems that emerge can develop more informal routines within or alongside the formal system.

These difficulties in implementing and maintaining such reward systems can give an indication of the lack of stability we may find in SME practices. At a recruitment business we worked with, there was a longstanding issue around performance-related pay. It was apparent from spending time in the business and with staff that the commission system changed on a regular basis. At one point it seemed that changes to how commission was calculated occurred on a quarterly basis. In the first quarter of the year consultants had been measured against a team target, but when this failed to produce the desired outcomes, the owner reverted to individual targets for the second quarter. When asked to explain how the latest pay arrangements would be used to calculate her performance-related earnings, one consultant apologised: 'Sorry I should be able to tell you that in more detail but it's changed three times [in the 12 months] since I've been here.'

Another explanation for the messy picture of SME practices might be found in how 'performance-related pay' is understood by study participants. Recalling Bacon *et al.*'s (1996) account of management practices in the hotel case study discussed in Chapter 5:

> A performance appraisal was 'I'll keep my eye on those that are not doing what they should, if someone does that bit extra and really helps us out then I'll slip them a bit more money in their pay packet'.
>
> (Bacon *et al.*, 1996: 88)

In other words, owner-managers in SMEs already play a central role in determining what employees get paid and part of this relates to their assessment of performance. To this extent, the pay arrangements could be considered performance related, even if not in the same way as the more formally structured approaches reported by larger organisations. Such informally granted rewards can be found throughout the research literature.

Reporting from Ghana, Debrah and Mmieh (2009) discuss how, in one of their case study firms, EduCo, the owner retained some retired and loyal employees on the business payroll. This 'private pension' was not granted to all former employees – only those who, in the owner's eyes, had served the company well over a number of years. Similar discretion applied to the allocation of housing for employees. In this way, it might be understood that some kind of performance-related reward arrangement can exist, albeit at the owner's discretion and without the typical associations with formal approaches to employment practices. More generally, financial benefits were available indirectly for teaching staff at EduCo. Although not possessing the formal qualifications required to teach in the state education sector, EduCo teaching staff could offer private lessons and their association with EduCo, even using the school premises for these activities, gave them good standing as private tutors.

### Task 6.1

Imagine you are an owner-manager of a small hotel that competes against international chains on the quality of service and affordable prices. How would you reward your employees? Why would you do it in this way? Discuss with a colleague to identify the potential strengths and weaknesses of your ideas.

Although such degrees of informality are not exclusive to SMEs (Ram *et al.*, 2001), relationships through which employees might be granted flexibility around working hours in return for effort or task flexibility (Nadin and Cassell,

2007; Tsai et al., 2007) can offer benefits to some employees. Unlike areas such as recruitment and selection, where the labour market might be seen as a dominant influence, here we might expect a clearer, more direct negotiation within the firm between employer and employees. However, as with all areas of people management in SMEs, there is a complex range of forces shaping reward and recognition practices.

## Shaping reward practices in SMEs

### *Owner-manager prerogative*

Owner-managers are often central figures in discussions of the pay arrangements found in SMEs, as with employment relationships and practices more generally. This focus can cast them as entrepreneurs and as targets of government policy and support, as the sole respondents in research identifying HRM practices in their firms or as the strategic heads of their organisations. The close social and spatial proximity that exists in many smaller firms can mean that owner-managers have direct involvement in all aspects of the business. In this sense SMEs have been viewed as an extension of the owner-manager's personality and subject to their wishes with this influence often seen as extended through the tendency towards informal management practices (Jennings and Beaver, 1997; Atkinson and Curtis, 2004; Marlow et al., 2010).

Whether their influence is discussed in terms of using discretion to set rates or hand out bonuses and other benefits, there can be a sense that owner-managers are able to exercise their prerogative over employees. Bonuses may not always be financial. In a paper we wrote with Carol Atkinson, we quote an owner-manager discussing his business' approach to areas such as paternity leave (Atkinson et al., 2014). He describes how awarding time off beyond regulatory requirements was seen as a form of reward extended, informally, by owner-manager prerogative:

> we have a fantastic sentence which goes at the end of everything, which is in the staff handbook, everybody's basic rights and legal rights are tried and at the end of it we have said this may be altered at the discretion of the directors. So, for example, the paternity leave, we just top it up to the full … But I'm not going to write it down that that is what we are going to do because, well, somebody really tried to take the mickey out of us. We want the flexibility of awarding it as a bonus really, so that's the flexibility.
> (Atkinson et al., 2014: 9)

While owner-managers are often able to exert considerable influence over matters in their businesses, it would be a mistake to assume such influence is necessarily absolute or applies in all circumstances (see Goss, 1991). In order to understand how this part of the employment relationship is shaped, we need to recall our discussion in Chapter 3 where we identified that multiple and interacting factors help to shape the particular sets of practices we might find in a given organisation at a particular point in time. To explore which factors seem to influence the reward and recognition practices associated with SMEs, and understand in what ways they have an influence, we will discuss, first, the external and then the internal environments that SMEs occupy. We hope that by reiterating this focus on both external and internal influences, we can help avoid creating an overly generalised understanding of 'what causes' reward practices to be as they are in SMEs in favour of a more questioning approach.

### External influences on reward in SMEs

If we consider reward and recognition in terms of Gilman and Edwards's framework (outlined in Chapter 3), we can begin to see some of the range of influences that contribute to owner-managers' decision-making processes and, potentially, constrain their ability to exert their prerogative. In this section we will consider three of the most influential external forces: regulation, labour market and product market. We will then move on to consider forms of influence inside the organisation.

*Regulation*

We will return to the topic of regulation in detail in Chapter 7, but in this chapter it is important to consider the role of minimum wage regulation and how it can affect SMEs. Regulation is interesting because it is often cited as a burden, depriving owner-managers of the freedom to operate their businesses as they see fit. As we explore later, popular discussions of regulation and SMEs are characterised by crude assumptions about its impact and the limited scope for smaller businesses to decide how they will respond to regulatory requirements.

Gilman et al. (2002) studied pay systems and the impacts of a specific piece of legislation, the national minimum wage (NMW – a rate of hourly pay that employers must meet or exceed), in three distinct sectors: hotels and catering, printing and clothing sectors. They view the introduction of NMW as an external shock affecting widely variable SME pay systems, albeit one that did not have the impact on jobs that had been expected by many when debating its introduction. They describe some of the impacts:

> Wider impacts depended on the ability of firms to absorb the increase in costs. Some were able to shift above the new legal minimum as a signal to improve recruitment and retention. Others sought to recoup the NMW by work intensification through closer supervision. A few companies had also sought to recover costs by withdrawing paid breaks ([hotels and catering]) or using more sophisticated forms of piecework (clothing) though for many the approach was rough-and-ready.
>
> (Gilman et al., 2002: 59)

In Gilman and colleagues' analysis, the advent of minimum wage legislation therefore served to add another consideration in how pay rates were arrived at. It did not have an automatic nor uniform effect on the businesses they studied. For now, then, we can acknowledge that regulation is an external influence that can have some bearing on pay levels and practices in SMEs. However, as we will see below, the nature of the impact that regulation has in particular firms can often depend on how they respond.

*Product market*

Rainnie's (1989) work on employment relations in small firms establishes that great significance is attributed to the influence of trading position relative to larger clients and rivals. As you will recall from Chapter 3, viewed in these terms, Rainnie argues that firms generally fall into one of four categories (see ibid.: 85), with each having implications for employment relationships within these firms. Commenting on the clothing sector of the UK economy, Rainnie suggests that in those firms which are in a dependent relationship with their client(s), there is:

> a pronounced diminution in the freedom of movement open to the individual owner/manager of small clothing factories. What is to be produced under what conditions and for how much are strictly laid down. Not only is management restricted in its options, but these self-same restrictions mean that little or no interference, from the workforce, could be tolerated.
> (Rainnie, 1989: 99)

Applying this to the case of pay within such firms, we might understand from Rainnie how the product market can exert a high degree of influence on the scope for owner-managers to organise their reward and recognition practices within a business. For example, small firms in sectors such as the clothing industry can become dependent upon large multinational chains, like supermarkets, which may insist on exclusivity for a certain product and then drive down the retail price, with implications for what the business can afford to pay its staff. Such is the size and power of these multinationals that owner-managers may find themselves powerless to resist and with little option in setting rates of pay.

*Labour market*

Returning to the work of Debrah and Mmieh (2009), we can see how labour market considerations might influence the organisation of rewards in some firms. The SMEs they studied in Ghana were constrained by operating relative to a high-paying state sector with which they could not compete. As a manager at EduCo described: 'Admittedly salaries are not competitive, we cannot compete with the government but we provide other incentives to retain employees' (ibid.: 1561). These 'other incentives' included Christmas gifts, parties and items of food.

In this context, where higher-paying alternative employment may be available to employees of a relatively under-resourced, low-paying SME, we can observe some of the attempts made to retain staff in a labour market disadvantageous to this business.

Another of Debrah and Mmieh's case study firms, AssureCo, operated in a very different environment of high unemployment, creating what was perceived as 'an employer's market' (Debrah and Mmieh, 2009: 1564). However, they still experienced shortages in particular staff roles. One response to this situation was for the CEO to exert their prerogative and unilaterally offer double the normal starting salary for a potential new recruit recommended by company managers. Elsewhere in the business, other benefits were not maintained as keenly, something employees acknowledged would have little effect on staff turnover rates considering the general economic context. What is interesting about the experience of AssureCo is that general labour market conditions did not have an even effect on the business. For some particular positions, the business encountered specific skills shortages and felt compelled to respond accordingly, while other areas were left unchanged.

As well as labour market considerations having uneven impacts on different parts of a business, the relation of a firm to the wider labour market can also be dynamic over time. From our own research, directors at a knowledge-intensive communications company established their business in a provincial university city, located away from rich pools of relevant talent. At first, the business benefited from being able to recruit junior members of staff locally on relatively low wages as graduates sought entry to the attractive PR and marketing field. However, as these employees became more skilled and more valuable owing to a scarcity of experienced talent in the local labour market, the business faced pressure to increase their wages or risk 'losing' those employees to other organisations in the area. In this way, the impacts of the labour market on the firm's approach to reward and recognition can change over time.

### Task 6.2

Choose three different types of SME. Drawing on Gilman and Edwards's framework, as set out in Chapter 3, consider in what ways external influences might shape arrangements for pay and rewards.

It would be an error to assume that external factors operate in isolation of each other or from other factors that we associate with the internal environment of SMEs. To avoid this error we need to consider the internal factors shaping reward and recognition in SMEs before we discuss how the different influences may interact to produce outcomes around reward and recognition practices in SMEs.

## Internal influences on reward in SMEs

As several of the studies discussed so far have indicated, management prerogative can play a significant role in the setting of rewards within a business. However, as we have seen with some of the external influences at work, such as regulations or powerful clients, this is not always the case. Similarly, we should not assume that employees are helpless, 'passive recipients of management control' (Ram and Edwards, 2003: 721) who are unable to negotiate their position. Gilman *et al.* (2002: 65) explain that:

> Pay arrangements reflected the external conditions of the labour and product markets, but also the informality of internal pay structures and scope for the adjustment of pay in the light of conceptions of fairness.

One of the key factors operating inside a firm that may influence or constrain owner-managers' actions is employees' idea of fairness, their perception of whether or not the systems in place, even if informal and ad hoc, are just.

### *Perceptions of justice*

Reporting on her study of pay systems in mostly medium-sized enterprises operating in the automotive engineering sector, Cox (2005) considered issues of justice. The analysis presented leads Cox to argue that focusing solely on whether outcomes are perceived to be fair risks missing broader considerations around procedural justice and the related concept of interactional justice. Procedural justice relates to *how* decisions about pay levels are made, while interactional justice is concerned with the way that procedures are followed – for instance, whether managers are perceived to follow the spirit of the procedures or are simply following them to the letter. This is particularly important when considering the relatively informal practices that operate in some SMEs. Cox's (2005) analysis of pay practices suggests that perceptions of justice or injustice can relate to a wide range of issues and, while rates of pay are an important consideration, these outcomes of management decisions cannot be separated from a wider understanding of how decisions are taken and implemented.

The type of complexity identified by Cox carries echoes of work by others who report that, from an employee perspective, perceptions of a fair deal in relation to the work done and rewards received are not just about high levels of pay. They form part of perceived rights and obligations for both employer and employees – what is sometimes discussed in the broader HRM literature in relation to a 'psychological contract' that must be considered alongside the more formal contract of employment (Atkinson *et al.*, 2014). Evidence presented by Arrowsmith *et al.* (2003), for example, suggests that employees in the restaurant trade had particular regard to the intensity of work required from them. While acknowledging that pay rates were low, this was to some extent balanced out by the work being seen as less stressful or demanding than alternative lines of work potentially available to the employees.

In small businesses we have worked with, perceptions of fairness or justice appeared to be complicated on occasion by the close social and spatial proximity of owner-manager and employees. While no one working at a financial services industry recruitment business ever questioned the right of the managing director to extract maximum profit from the business, funding a lifestyle that included a £100,000 sports car, this contrasted with the directors at other firms who reported personal concerns that staff were making regular calculations along the lines of: Revenues Generated *minus* Employee Salaries *equals* What the Owners Must be Making.

At a different recruitment business, the managing director complained about staff requests for more money, contrasting his perceptions of their attitude with his memories of working for a global blue-chip organisation:

> I don't know whether it's something particular to small firms – basically no one ever bothered with that at [blue chip]. You didn't think 'where's my share?' when you heard predictions of the organisation making over £3bn that year.
>
> I used to get my car bills [leasing] sent home because I didn't want people thinking 'Oh, he spends more on a car each month than I get paid', but now I let them see it. It's important to look professional, have something that's reliable, safe ... I drive [model of car] a good, midrange car, no better than I had at [blue chip] so ... my view is that's the way of the world.

Perceptions of justice and of the upholding of a psychological contract also have important implications for both the procedural fairness of administering a reward and recognition system as well as the outputs of that system (for instance, the rates of pay received). For example, in Carol Atkinson's (2008) paper on psychological contracts within medium-sized firms and the trust between employers and employees, she identifies pay as the most salient obligation for employees. Atkinson quotes a machine operative at one of her case study firms as explaining the violation of a perceived obligation on the part of their employer:

> In general, I think the worst thing that has happened here in the last 4 or 5 years, is that we haven't had one pay rise. You get inflation, I know it's pretty low, but it's still not gone ... In the mid-90s they made millions this company, and we never got nothing. Because things have gone wrong, we still get nothing ... We've had nothing at all for the last five years ... That's the biggest bugbear.
>
> (Atkinson, 2008: 457)

What is important in terms of our present discussion around factors influencing reward and recognition is the impacts of these perceptions of unfairness or injustice. This can be seen in the discomfort felt by some owner-managers around employee perceptions of their own remuneration. However, the impacts go much further than a sense of discomfort. Where such perceptions of unfairness or injustice persist, they can lead to disputes and ongoing forms of negotiation that may exist both within and outside formal pay-setting procedures.

*Sources of power and influence*

We should never assume, even in non-unionised, owner-manager-dominated small firms, that employees are helpless in the face of management prerogative. There are potential limits to owner-manager prerogative within any firm. These limits may relate to a desire for stability, such that the costs in time and resources of replacing a member of staff may grant some power and influence to existing, effective employees. There are other potential sources of influence too, such as those relating to skill sets, networks or tacit knowledge that can mean an employee can be difficult to replace and therefore exert a degree of influence, for example in areas relating to their specific expertise or where an owner-manager comes to rely upon them.

It is also important not to discount the informality, social proximity and the relationships that can develop in small firms and, in some cases, pre-exist the firm altogether. As discussed in Chapter 4, firms do not always recruit in an open labour market but may recruit friends and family or other people already known to the business. Such people may exert forms of influence derived from sources outside of the employment relationship. For example, in Marlow *et al.*'s (2010) account of life at HaulCo, the daughter of the finance director decided that a new employee was, in fact, a white witch! After her lobbying successfully for this employee's dismissal, the business then spent money removing traces of the employee having ever worked there.

Sources of power and influence are therefore complex and, potentially, unpredictable. They can relate to external factors such as the labour or product markets, but also to interpersonal relationships within the firm. Some of these complexities will become clearer as we move on to discuss forms of negotiation around reward and recognition in SMEs.

*Ongoing, everyday negotiation*

As we have seen, the factors affecting reward and recognition are dynamic, varying in their effects within and between firms as well as over time. Similarly, the internal negotiations, around issues such as additional rewards beyond standard rates of pay, are often ongoing. They can relate to explicit, formal negotiations, such as requesting a pay rise or additional recognition for high performance, but also informal and, possibly, implicit forms of negotiation that we will outline below.

Concerned by his company's declining performance against client service-level agreements, yet still paying commission for placements, the owner-manager of a recruitment firm we analysed in Wapshott and Mallett (2013) had become frustrated with his employees. Eventually, he opted to overhaul his company's commission scheme completely, redesigning it explicitly in line with his current goals. The changes increased emphasis on client satisfaction, and while winning new business would attract a higher rate of commission, the relatively easy work of filling vacancies at existing clients would receive reduced rates. Acting in a unilateral fashion and designing the new system without employee consultation, the owner-manager exercised his prerogative.

The consultants learned of the change at an implementation meeting. As the operations manager told us, initial reactions were not positive:

INTERVIEWEE: Well, Kathy cried.
RW: Cried?
INTERVIEWEE: Yes, she actually excused herself [from the meeting] and cried in the office. Lucy got mad ... anyway, she was off sick all the time.

Although the changes might reduce consultant earnings, other performance-related rewards were offered. However, the consultants focused on those changes that, they argued, would cost them hundreds of pounds each month in lost commission. Three weeks after the announcement, the owner-manager described the atmosphere as 'a bit Frosty the Snowman', and within a couple of months his changes had been quietly dropped.

The previous system had been gradually adapted through an implicit process of mutual adjustment and was deeply embedded in the employee's perceptions of the psychological contract. In redesigning this pay system, the owner-manager had failed to acknowledge the potential power held by those at the heart of his business, assuming that, as owner, he had the prerogative to set pay and commission rates unilaterally. However, when those resistant employees eventually left the firm (through unrelated causes), the owner-manager found that, contrary to his previous fears, replacing them was relatively easy and caused minimal disruption to clients. Accordingly, he felt confident in reintroducing the previously abandoned reward scheme. New employees, with none of the history of negotiation and with a different sense of their rights and obligations, expressed little resistance and accepted the scheme without incident.

While owner-managers might seek to exert their prerogative in setting rewards and recognition, we should not see employee resistance as impossible, even if, in some circumstances, it may be difficult. In particular, while studies of small firms have examined the informal nature of negotiation shaping employment relationships (Holliday, 1995), limited attention has been given to illuminating other ways in which employment relationships and working practices might develop. These negotiated outcomes can be informed by less explicit processes, forming part of the mutual adjustment that occurs in employment relationships (Ram, 1994; Holliday, 1995; Moule, 1998). By the term 'mutual adjustment', we mean the processes through which owner-managers and employees accommodate, adapt to and potentially struggle with one another in developing the employment relationships and practices existing in an organisation. In negotiating the rights and obligations within the psychological contract, both employers and employees will concede ground necessary to achieve their goals. Furthermore, these negotiations feature degrees of what we term 'intersubjective negotiation' (Wapshott and Mallett, 2013: 988) which can prove particularly influential in relatively informal organisations.

Through processes of intersubjective negotiation, employers and employees adjust their relative positions by 'second-guessing' what the other is thinking about. Intersubjectivity is derived from the interactional infrastructure of organisations in which individuals seek to understand others, to make themselves understood and to hold one another accountable for these understandings (Reich, 2010). Approaches to conceptualising the employment relationship such as the psychological contract can be considered as relating to *perceptions* of what rights and obligations exist within the organisation and violation may only be apparent to one party in the 'contract'. It will often be perceptions of factors such as procedural justice, rights and obligations or of external factors such as the labour market that influence people's bargaining positions and sense of security or threat, strength or weakness.

For example, if an employee perceives themselves as having rights to particular benefits that are withdrawn by an employer who saw them as temporary or unsatisfactory, or if an employer perceives difficulties in replacing key members of staff (as at the recruitment firm discussed above), such issues may not be dealt with explicitly but still influence the shaping of reward and recognition systems and the broader employment relationship. These perceptions, and others, have an important influence on the processes of negotiation within the firm. The employer who perceives a threat of staff leaving for higher-paid roles elsewhere may not ask the staff about their intentions, but instead introduce some new bonus or other form of financial recognition aimed at securing the loyalty of these employees and based upon a set of assumptions about what will be required to secure the owner-manager's goals. Intersubjectivity is therefore a vital part of the inter-relational nature of organisations, reflecting the importance of our perception of someone else's perceptions, our taking-into-account of their subjective interpretations and experience.

The role of such intersubjective negotiations has not received much attention in the literature (Wapshott and Mallett, 2013). However, the reliance of owner-managers on their personal assessments (Nooteboom, 1988), discussions of tacit understanding and knowledge management (Edwards, 2007; Edwards *et al.*, 2007; Yu, 2009) and the role of individual subjectivity in relational development (Jayasinghe *et al.*, 2008), have suggested something of the idea's relevance. In relation to external influences such as the labour market, the distorting effects of owner-manager perceptions (an owner-manager will not have an objective, wholly accurate grasp of the labour market or its implications for their firm), and the ongoing negotiations fed into by these perceptions, help to explain some of the different effects such influences can have in different firms (see, for example, Sharifi and Zhang, 2009, on the relative unimportance of truth in the negotiation of organisational definitions).

## *The interaction of external and internal factors*

SME practices are produced through a mix of external and internal influences. While commentators may vary on the degree of emphasis attributed to the influence of external factors over internal considerations (Moule, 1998), there is broad consensus around the need for understanding the scope for decisions to be made within the firm, even in the face of significant external pressures (Ram and Edwards, 2003).

A good example of the limitations of even powerful external influences is found in the work of Arrowsmith *et al.* (2003), building on their earlier work (Gilman *et al.*, 2002), discussed earlier, which explored small firms and the introduction in the UK of an NMW. The introduction of legislation, such as that mandating minimum hourly rates of pay or maximum hours worked per week (the 'working time directive'), represents a government seeking to influence directly employment relationships and practices within businesses. However, as Arrowsmith and his colleagues demonstrate with their longitudinal analysis of 55 firms, even this powerful, external influence will interact with other factors within the firm and, as a result, produce variable outcomes between different firms – even those of similar size and within the same sector.

This research looked at two sectors (clothing manufacture and hotels and catering) and identified key challenges the firms faced such as, for example, 'only a quarter of affected companies felt able to pass on the increase in costs through higher prices' (Arrowsmith *et al.*, 2003: 441). However, for each sector, evidence was found for three broad types of response being made to this new legislation. The observation that even in the face of national legislation, operators in similar lines of business chose either to *implement, ignore* or treat the new regulations as a *critical event* about which to reflect more widely, indicates the scope for internal adjustment to external factors. Clearly, not many firms are likely to admit to ignoring the NMW rules but there were very different ways in which some firms adapted to comply with what they identified as the minimum requirements. Arrowsmith *et al.* (2003: 444) provide the following example:

INTERVIEWER: 'How much do the staff earn?'
CO-OWNER: 'They earn £90 to £95 a week.'
INTERVIEWER: 'How many hours is that for?'
CO-OWNER: 'Work it out for yourself – it's that amount divided by £3.60.
  [where this was the minimum wage in force at the time]'

Statements such as this would appear to suggest the possibility that employees' pay may have been unaltered by the introduction of the regulations but the number of hours they were recorded as working each week decreased, irrespective of their actual hours worked, to ensure their pay met the legal minimum. In effect, the introduction of an NMW that could, in some circumstances, mean such staff were now better off, meant simply working additional, unpaid overtime.

Beyond simply ignoring, or attempting to ignore, the law, there are further ways in which external influences will be interpreted and enacted in different ways within different businesses. Arrowsmith *et al.* (2003: 449) explain:

> The small firms in the research were not only at the mercy of the product market, which in any case placed a premium on maintaining stability in the workplace, but also were subject to more or less intense labour market pressures. Low margins helped keep pay relatively low, leaving working time vital to recruitment and retention. This meant that there was a large variation in practices, including in wages and working time patterns, even in the same product markets and geographical areas.

However, despite instances of internal negotiation, Arrowsmith and his colleagues, who interviewed employees as well as employers, reported frequent instances of employees feeling powerless and employers feeling free to act as they wanted. It is therefore important not to forget owner-manager prerogative, even while we suggest its limitations. As Arrowsmith *et al.* (2003: 450) report:

> Significantly, pay-setting was usually an issue for management alone. Three-quarters of hotel and catering workers, and four-fifths of those in clothing, said their employer decided the increase unilaterally, with only one in five and one in ten respectively reporting some discussion and an even smaller minority saying they had a significant say.

Thus, while these figures may not include the types of implicit, intersubjective forms of influence and negotiation we discussed earlier in the chapter, owner-manager prerogative can heavily influence practices in SMEs and, importantly, the ways in which these practices are perceived by employees.

### Task 6.3

At the start of this chapter we presented a comment from Cardon and Stevens (2004) on the apparent lack of systematic and rational approaches to reward assumed to exist in SMEs. In light of what you have considered during this chapter, why is it perhaps unfair to present these practices as simply not systematic and not rational?

## Conclusion

The topic of reward and recognition in SMEs has been discussed to explore this aspect of employment relationships and practices in SMEs alongside broader considerations of power and negotiation. This is important if we are to develop our understanding of the tensions between control and autonomy that exist in many SMEs. We have considered how, while owner-managers can exert significant influence through their prerogative, this should not be interpreted as the only or necessarily dominant influence at work. Notwithstanding the centrality of owner-manager prerogative, in understanding how rates of pay, or rewards and recognition more generally, are established we can see that various factors come into play. These factors, and the interactions between them, create certain opportunities and challenges for those who manage SMEs as well as those working within them. The complexities that may resolve themselves, at least temporarily, in management practices and employee performance serve as a reminder to consider the context of the businesses being studied before reaching for generalised conclusions or assumptions about how reward and recognition operate. The different outcomes of interactions between external and internal influences, ongoing, everyday negotiations and forms of intersubjective mutual adjustment give us some important insights into the heterogeneity of SMEs. For example, they explain why legislation, such as that mandating a national minimum wage, will exhibit great variation in its impacts on individual businesses.

Writing from a similar perspective, Verreynne *et al.* (2013: 424) draw out implications for how firms are studied, arguing that, 'CEO-centric research approaches leave those with the greatest insight outside the research frame'. We will return to this insight in Chapter 9. It also reminds us to consider the breadth of potential influences, not just on reward and recognition, but also employment relationships and practices more generally. Negotiating in response to a variety of challenges, some more or less relevant to firms in different and dynamic contexts, may give a sense that things are not 'systematic', but describing these responses as irrational (Cardon and Stevens, 2004) is unhelpful. We suggest that it is more useful to consider not just the outcomes, in terms of the practices in use, but also *how* and *why* these practices emerge before passing judgement on them.

# 7   Staff turnover

People can leave an organisation for a range of reasons, including voluntary staff departure, but more often than not the focus of the academic literature (and politicians' speeches) is placed on dismissal – particularly unfair dismissal. The topic of staff exit and turnover is one that excites extensive discussion and is often related to debates around the legal regulation of employment in SMEs. This chapter will explore staff turnover in cases of voluntary and involuntary exit, including a discussion of managing poor performance. In this context, we will also explore the influence of Employment Tribunals and forms of regulation on influencing management practices within SMEs and critique the public debates around over-regulation of employment in SMEs.

## Voluntary staff turnover

In their paper 'Job mobility restriction mechanisms and appropriability in organizations: the mediating role of secrecy and lead time', Delerue and Lejeune (2010) report on a study of biotechnology firms employing fewer than 250 people. The authors explain how, in research-intensive environments:

> Voluntary turnover often results in the hiring of departing employees by competing firms, creating an even more critical situation, since their knowledge can now be used against the organization. Labor mobility poses a potential threat to the firm because its R&D [research and development] capital is embodied in its employees.
> 
> (Delerue and Lejeune, 2010: 360)

In certain types of work there might, therefore, be significant risks of key employees leaving for a rival business or setting up their own venture following an important discovery in the course of their employment. In the previous chapter we discussed situations where employees may have a stronger negotiating position owing to their value to the organisation. Here we find knowledge-intensive workers whose exit would not only cause direct problems but, further, benefit rival businesses. The real or perceived threat of staff turnover may, for certain firms, therefore act as a powerful check on owner-manager prerogative, as discussed in Chapter 6.

Voluntary turnover is generally regarded as a negative event for small organisations because it may be that 'most of a small company's assets reside in human capital' (Patel and Conklin, 2012: 208). This means that when staff leave, the business could be losing some of the attributes on which it trades. For businesses that rely on the knowledge and skills of their employees, such as professional service firms, voluntary staff turnover poses a number of problems that can hamper the success of that business (Drummond and Stone, 2007). An immediate practical concern can arise in the business having sufficient resources to deliver existing contracts and meet the demands of its clients. With relatively few staff, small businesses may have limited capacity to cover gaps in their workforce. Further, where staff possess knowledge of a business innovation or strategy, they can undermine any potential competitive advantage these might deliver by taking that knowledge to a rival employer. Turnover of certain staff can therefore hamper the capacity of some businesses to build for their future.

Still, the potential damage caused by voluntary staff turnover is not only limited to the technical ability or knowledge of a business. There are social aspects to consider too in how a business relates to important clients. Drummond and Stone (2007) report on consultancy businesses that operated in fiercely competitive labour markets. While the skills and knowledge of their specialist employees were essential, the business owners also recognised that their consultants played a vital role in maintaining client relationships for the business. They were conscious that should a consultant leave the business, their clients might follow them, compounding the negative impact. Such turnover might not only affect clients who were served directly by a particular employee, but could also communicate a negative message to other clients. In our own research, we came across examples of business owners being reluctant to communicate staff changes for fear of clients becoming unsettled at a lack of stability. Some clients were expressing concerns about the levels of staff turnover at the service provider and sought assurances that quality and service levels would be maintained.

While high-skilled sectors might experience severe consequences of voluntary turnover among the very people who create value in a business, enterprises in other sectors can also encounter difficulties from staff turnover. As discussed in Chapter 4, Martin *et al.* (2006) report on the problems of the Scottish tourism industry. Despite representing somewhere in the region of £4.5 billion worth of revenue (or 5% of Scotland's GDP at the time of the research), the Scottish tourism industry is hampered by unusually high levels of staff turnover. Perceptions of the industry as not offering a 'serious career' (ibid.: 385), compounding low rates of pay and poor development opportunities, can be reinforced by evidence of high staff turnover at entry and managerial levels of employment. High turnover across an entire industry might, therefore, portray the sector as an undesirable career path and work against efforts to attract graduates or others with the skills and experience to develop an important part of the national economy.

This problem can be seen more generally where, as Schlosser (2015) argues, SMEs can struggle to find replacement staff, particularly to fill key roles, owing to perceptions of limited opportunities for advancement and the potential for risk of business failure. As discussed in Chapter 4, SMEs may not be perceived as a first-choice organisation to work for and build a career (Williamson, 2000), and outside their established networks SMEs might struggle to attract the best staff. Even where suitable staff can be recruited, there remain issues around staff training and, in certain industries, the lead time required for new recruits to acquire the necessary tacit knowledge to perform as required (Drummond and Stone, 2007).

There are, therefore, important implications for some businesses following staff exit. Writing about the construction industry in China, Gao et al. (2013) are interested primarily in risk management but offer two interesting examples of how staff turnover can affect SMEs. In the first instance they report problems of increasing capacity around risk management within the workforce. With high levels of turnover, the business had limited numbers of staff who understood risk management and were able to transfer this expertise to new recruits. In this way, additional pressures are created for the recruitment of new staff and the provision of, potentially, more formal and expensive external training and development. A range of pressures, then, can impact upon the firms and their resources following staff exit.

Reflecting on this issue in the context of the materials discussed in Chapter 5, we might see an interesting problem arise. With high voluntary staff turnover, a business might not invest in formal training assuming that the investment will 'exit' the business. The training is therefore left in the hands of informal, on-the-job approaches. In contexts of very high voluntary staff turnover, however, a point might be reached when there is insufficient knowledge residing in the workforce to train new recruits adequately on informal lines. We might, therefore, reach a point in very high turnover environments where it makes sense to codify the required knowledge systematically and permit increased levels of formal training, simply in order for the business to function in this environment.

Away from the considerations of the building site, Gao et al. (2013) report how the business owners, and some employees, had close social or family links with local government officials with oversight for regulatory enforcement. Gao et al. report one group head as explaining:

> If there is a problem in terms of compliance with regulations, we can always find a friend from the authorities to help us. Particularly as we have very good connections with the local government, we can easily get away with many regulations and requirements.
>
> (Gao et al., 2013: 687)

Such strong ties to local decision makers in the sometimes contentious environment of property development in China could prove valuable. If we step back a little from the detail of Gao et al.'s study and think about a situation in which a particular employee, rather than a number of them, held such relationships, it is clear that a great deal could be at stake should that employee leave the business.

## Staff retention

If voluntary staff turnover can present a major problem for SMEs, it raises the question of whether these businesses can do anything to retain the staff they have and wish to keep. Before we get into a discussion of how businesses can potentially limit staff turnover, it is important to take a step back and acknowledge that not all voluntary staff turnover is caused by issues that relate to someone's job or workplace. Reflecting on Perrow's (1970: 52) observation of organisations generally that '[t]he organization is not the total world of the individual; it is not a society', we should appreciate how staff turnover might relate to events in people's lives away from their workplace. For example, health concerns might arise that make continuing to work for an employer impractical or a spouse might take a new job that requires relocation, especially as many SMEs may be tied to one site. Likewise, decisions to remain with an employer in a particular location might be influenced by issues in someone's personal life as much as job considerations or commitment to an employer. With this in mind, the potential for successful staff retention may be limited. In this section, we focus on issues within the organisation.

### *Available alternatives*

Where the question of whether to leave a business relates primarily to experiences within that organisation, Allen *et al.* (2013, drawing on the work of Shaw *et al.*, 1998) suggest that this depends on the attraction to stay set against the availability of alternatives. This distinction is helpful in trying to understand differences in job mobility. On the basis that, for voluntary turnover, an employee must have certain attributes that make alternative employment a viable option, we can start by considering the availability of alternatives.

Employees with attributes that are in demand from employers may become aware of this demand and the opportunities associated with it. This returns us to the important ways in which the external labour market can influence employment relationships within SMEs, but also the need for employer or employee understanding of this labour market. For example, in Chris Smith's (2006) conceptual discussion, 'The double indeterminacy of labour power: labour effort and labour mobility', he identifies how the very nature of some jobs played a role in providing opportunities for employee mobility:

> Attending conferences in working time, for example, is essential to the work of many professional groups, such as medics, scientists, engineers, academics etc., and these are used, often explicitly, as hiring halls.
>
> (Smith, 2006: 391)

Within such environments, sharing information on the opportunities available across a given industry and making informal approaches to potential hires is straightforward. We might encounter similar situations with professionals who provide services to a client and that client later offers them a permanent in-house role as part of their organisation. Of course, not all jobs feature this kind of networking with potential employers. Jobs that are based in single locations, such as factories or offices, which do not require much interaction with members of other organisations who could offer alternative employment, clearly do not facilitate acquiring knowledge of available alternatives in the same way.

The availability of alternative job opportunities, or even the (mistaken) belief on behalf of an employer that such opportunities exist (Wapshott and Mallett, 2013), raises the question of how attractive it is to stay within the current business. Working environments that are characterised by factors such as relatively low levels of stress, identification with organisational values and goals, opportunities for career progression and a strong group culture may prove highly attractive to employees and so encourage retention (Ahmed and Chowdhury, 2009; Pajo et al., 2010; Patel and Conklin, 2012; Saridakis et al., 2013). Where such characteristics are not present, the attractiveness of staying in the face of available opportunities for alternative employment elsewhere might prove insufficient.

## Ongoing, everyday negotiation

As we have discussed throughout the book, and in detail in Chapter 6, employment relationships are the product of negotiations. In the face of perceived disparity between the attractiveness of a current job, as against what may be available to employees were they to leave, employers might seek to improve their offer to certain employees (Wapshott and Mallett, 2013). This may result in enhanced benefits, such as flexible working patterns, but it also impacts investments in employees, as we discussed in terms of training and development in Chapter 5, where employers do not want to train employees to the point where they can get a 'better' job elsewhere. Such calculations between employers and employees can continue on an ongoing, everyday basis with little explicit acknowledgement between the parties that they are engaged in a form of negotiation.

This negotiated order of workplaces (see Ram, 1994) also influences day-to-day interactions and discipline. In the case of ButtonCo, Moule (1998) describes how unscheduled smoking breaks among staff were common. For the relatively less-skilled despatch workers, getting caught by a director typically led to a rebuke, whereas for dyehouse workers central to the company's productive capacity, 'proprietorial tolerance appeared greater; tacit recognition perhaps of the central role which dyers played in the success of the company' (ibid.: 674). In organisations lacking formal policies, or their consistent application, variable practices therefore emerge where the threat or danger of staff exit can be a key determining factor. In light of such ongoing negotiations, the relative attractiveness of staying put set against the availability of alternatives can be shifting, dynamic territory that never quite settles.

**Good turnover?**

There is a tendency within the research literature that addresses employment or HRM issues in SMEs to view voluntary turnover as a necessarily bad thing for organisations. In part, this derives from the problems associated with staff turnover identified by Patel and Conklin (2012) above, but it also reflects how staff turnover is rather bluntly framed in studies of high performance work systems generally associated with much larger organisations than SMEs (which is a broader topic we will return to in Chapter 9); low levels of staff turnover are treated as an indicator of effective human resource management (Sheehan, 2014). To develop a contrasting viewpoint, we might consider what happens to those who lack viable and available alternatives elsewhere in the jobs market. Where these employees are satisfied there may be little consequence for their employer, but where these employees are dissatisfied and find themselves 'stuck' in an organisation, staff 'retention' might become a problem. The retention of unhappy, dissatisfied and unproductive staff unable to leave the organisation has the potential to cause debilitating effects, especially in small firms with close spatial and social proximity. However, in some industries, striking a balance between voluntary turnover and staff retention can prove particularly tricky.

When we studied a creative design business we encountered the management team's ongoing tension regarding experienced and long-serving employees. While the managers stressed that they valued their long-serving designers, at the same time they wondered whether they could benefit from some degree of staff turnover through which fresh blood could boost creativity. Despite the skills possessed by experienced designers, they were not perceived as closely aligned with some of the target markets the business was tasked with reaching:

> In a way retention's been a disadvantage recently in [head office] because the design team, they've all been there for so long. You get sort of an inverted pyramid, very heavyweight designers with lots of experience and a company like this needs lots of young people with new ideas. The leadership team is ... around late 30s early 40s, not old people but ... we're not 20, 21, 22 kicking out of art college and we're sometimes communicating brands which are appealing to those people so it's actually very beneficial to have a throughput of people.

Staff turnover has the potential to stimulate new working practices as the organisation adjusts to cover the gaps or, with the hiring of replacement staff, to bring new knowledge into the organisation. Similarly, in studying biotechnology SMEs, Delerue and Lejeune (2010) observe how tensions arise in organisations that benefit creatively through attracting staff from other organisations but, at the same time, must work hard at protecting their own intellectual property and innovations. Staff retention is therefore a complex matter and, as we will see in the next section, challenges relating to retention and exit can be heightened by the informal and ad hoc practices that dominate some SMEs.

## Involuntary staff exit

Involuntary turnover is a rather dry description for staff redundancies or lay-offs. It is a topic that, especially in relation to employment regulation and tribunals, receives significant political attention among small business lobby groups and political parties, inevitably simplifying nuances of the issues to make broad points. Popular calls for reductions in employment regulation often focus on how it dampens enthusiasm among employers for taking on new staff for fear they cannot later dismiss them, but the research evidence is more complicated than this.

### Formal policies and informal practice

A paper by Cho *et al.* (2011), titled 'Dismissal law and human resource management in SMEs: lessons from Korea', highlights some of the complexities of involuntary staff turnover in relation to informal practices in SMEs. They explore changes in South Korea following financial assistance from the International Monetary Fund, part of the terms for which included forms of deregulation that made it easier for firms to terminate employee contracts. As the paper describes:

> Employers supported this deregulatory trend wholeheartedly, and argued that this greater freedom to make employment adjustments would enhance competitiveness, thereby creating more jobs and thus, eventually, benefitting employees.
>
> (Cho *et al.*, 2011: 106)

Cho and colleagues describe the implications for SMEs of the new dismissal law, which they identify as principally made manifest in increased rates of unfair dismissal. They explain this increase in terms of the financial pressures faced by SMEs during a financial crisis, a lack of union representation but also, in part, a misinterpretation of the rules and their implementation within the firms.

Cho *et al.* suggest that the new legislation was not entirely clear and was often poorly translated into policy and practice, leading to owner-managers believing they had greater scope to exercise their prerogative in dismissals than they in fact did. In response to these problems, some employers are reported to have found ways to avoid the complexities of the dismissal regulations, for example by employing short-tenured staff or subcontractors. Ultimately, the change in the law did not meet its objectives, in part due to failing to appreciate the everyday realities of SME practices.

Many SMEs will have formal policies to follow in case of disciplinary action and dismissal, especially due to fears owner-managers can have about the complexity of regulations and the dangers of claims for unfair dismissal. As a result, formal policies may be designed by external legal consultants and advisers (Atkinson *et al.*, 2014; Kitching, 2015). However, as we have seen in other areas of human resource management throughout this book, SMEs can often revert to informal, ad hoc practices, even where formal policies, such as those to ensure regulatory compliance, are in place.

As part of a report for the British government's Department for Business Innovation and Skills, Jordan *et al.* (2013) conducted research into employer perceptions of the impacts of employment regulation. They indicate that with small and micro businesses, problems can arise through a reluctance to instigate formal processes to tackle poorly performing employees. Participants in their study believed that initiating formal measures would affect personal relationships in the business. Consequently, these employers would only start formal procedures against an employee once a decision to dismiss them had been taken. Jordan *et al.* (2013) argue that not only does this deprive both parties of a chance to resolve the problems, but the informal, quiet word approach also leaves the employer struggling to demonstrate that they gave the employee sufficient opportunity to improve their conduct as required.

While there are perceived benefits to organising employment relationships along relatively informal lines in smaller businesses, when those relationships sour formal policies and practices have an important role to play. Even though SMEs are less likely than large businesses to have claims for unfair dismissal brought against them, when legal claims reach a full Employment Tribunal hearing small businesses have been found to be more likely than medium-sized and large businesses to lose (Saridakis *et al.*, 2008). Given the political prominence of these tribunals, and the fear they provoke in some owner-managers, it is a topic worth considering in detail.

### SMEs and Employment Tribunals

Acas (the Advisory, Conciliation and Arbitration Service) is a UK agency tasked with resolving disputes within employment relationships, and provides advice, support and conciliation services (and must be engaged with before proceeding to legal action in such a dispute). They define an Employment Tribunal as follows:

> The Employment Tribunals are an independent judicial body established to resolve disputes between employers and employees over employment rights. The tribunal will hear claims about employment matters such as unfair dismissal, discrimination, wages and redundancy payments.
>
> Employment Tribunals are less formal than a court, for example no one wears a wig or gown. However, like a court, tribunals cannot give out

legal advice, almost all hearings are open to the public, and evidence will be given under oath or affirmation.

(www.acas.org.uk/index.aspx?articleid=1889)

Saridakis *et al.* (2008) suggest that to understand the relatively highly likelihood for small firms to lose at these types of tribunal, we need an appreciation of how the 'formality' operating within small firms differs from that expected within a legal context. As a result of these differences, once at the hearing, small firms:

> are likely to find that their interpretation of procedural propriety differs from that of the Tribunal, and that what is reasonable in their own terms, for example, having the same manager dismiss a worker and hear an appeal, may not stand up to scrutiny.
>
> (Saridakis *et al.*, 2008: 493)

That is, often lacking integrated policies and managers who have been specifically tasked with ensuring compliance, SMEs may not be as rigorously engaged with their obligations and formal processes as larger firms. Further, we know that in certain aspects of SME employment relationships, such as Investors in People accreditation (see Chapter 5), policies can exist for status purposes without really changing practices within a business. This 'empty shell' (Hoque and Noon, 2004) approach to policy in SMEs is accepted as being par for the course, but in the context of employment regulation, it can represent a problem. Edwards *et al.* (2004) draw on evidence from the UK Workplace Employment Relations Study (1998) to indicate that 70% of the small firms surveyed had a formal disciplinary procedure in place but, clearly, businesses need to *follow* these procedures if they are to make a difference (Saridakis *et al.*, 2008).

Even when followed, however, there remains scope for management discretion over how procedures are enacted. Regulatory compliance and adhering to a perceived higher standard of fairness can be distinct. In an article we wrote with Carol Atkinson, drawing on her PhD research into the psychological contract and employment relationships in medium-sized firms (Atkinson *et al.*, 2014), we discuss an interesting case of apparent compliance that, under further scrutiny, may actually represent the exertion of informal owner-manager prerogative. In the paper we cite the case of TechCo, as related by a software developer:

> Well, I don't think they were quite as open as they said. On the second set of redundancies they had a scoring system ... it was supposed to be fair where it evaluated the person. There was a set of criteria basically, so like what skills a person had, how flexible they were, how much this person bought into the company principles and so on. And I don't honestly believe that those scores were the basis for making people redundant. I believe they had already targeted who they wanted to get rid of and then manipulated the scores.
>
> (Atkinson *et al.*, 2014: 12)

Although the employees of the business seemed content that the company procedures and legal requirements had been adhered to, there was a sense that employers had overlooked more interpersonal, informal obligations they had towards their employees. This example may go some way to suggesting that both management practices in relation to employment law and in particular to staff exit, as well as employee evaluations of such actions, may not simply reflect 'objective', formal legal requirements but must still be situated and interpreted as part of informal, ongoing (employment) relationships between people. In this way, though not specifically in relation to this particular firm, formal policies that appear compliant may, under the scrutiny of an Employment Tribunal, not meet the standards required to avoid damages for unfair dismissal.

## The negotiation of regulatory compliance

We have touched on regulation several times as a powerful external influence, for example in relation to the influence of a national minimum wage (NMW) on reward and recognition, but discussed how such forces can influence practices in more complex ways than one might expect. In these ways, the tone of political debates, with repeated references to 'red tape' stifling enterprise becoming part of the accepted terms of the discussion, is often unhelpful in really understanding how regulation influences employment relations in SMEs. It is therefore worth considering regulation and SMEs in relation to the light this can throw on formal policies, such as those relating to disciplinary processes and employee dismissal, and the ways they can interact with informal, everyday practices.

As we have discussed, for example in Chapter 6, SMEs are often considered to be dominated by the interests and goals of their owner-managers (Scott *et al.*, 1989; Jennings and Beaver, 1997). Owner-managers are therefore often the target of regulatory interventions, debates and research projects. They generally express a dislike for any measures that could interfere with their managerial prerogative (Westrip, 1986; Wilkinson, 1999; Atkinson and Curtis, 2004), in line with a general preference for informal employment relationships (Marlow, 2003). Their dissatisfaction tends to highlight compliance costs, which are argued to affect smaller businesses disproportionately in several ways (see Carter *et al.*, 2009), such as the costs and disruption of changing business practices. As Harris (2000) argues, one of the main difficulties small firms encounter with respect to regulation is an inability to adapt as regulations change.

The full impacts of regulation are difficult to identify or understand, they are not only straightforward and direct but dynamic and, at times, indirect (Kitching, 2006; Atkinson *et al.*, 2014). In considering their question of 'Why does employment legislation not damage small firms?' Edwards *et al.* (2004) identify three sources of influence on how employment regulations might impact small firms:

1  *Filtering effects*: how deeply embedded legal requirements are into practice, the negotiated employment relationship and the firm's economic context

will affect the firm's ability to absorb compliance costs, filtering the effects of regulation.

2   *Relevance effects*: how relevant a particular law or piece of regulation is to a firm will vary, leading to:

- Direct effects: the regulatory requirements are implemented by the firm.
- Indirect effects: the regulation requires some action to be taken but the action to be taken is not mandated.
- Affinity effects: a firm changes its internal practices in the spirit of a perceived general trend in regulation, even though the laws do not require action from the firm.

3   *Knock-on effects*: further effects may result from the initial changes made to ensure compliance.

(Adapted from Edwards *et al.*, 2004: 250–2)

Importantly, these types of effect can be positive or negative and will not, therefore, necessarily have the damaging effects often claimed by the more hysterical reports of business advocacy groups. For example, some effects of compliance could bring improvements to a given business, such as in the form of increased efficiencies as it seeks to cope with, or mitigate, the effects of cost increases owing to new regulatory requirements.

Edwards *et al.* (2004: 255) illustrate the core of their argument with the story of a care home, where they spoke to the owner-managers:

> Their initial response to us was to state that 'we'll show how badly the regulations are affecting us', citing the NMW and the Working Families Tax Credit as examples. Yet deeper investigation revealed that the NMW had led to pay rises from £4.20 to between £4.50 and £4.75; the WTR [working time regulations] necessitated no new record-keeping and there was no experience of maternity or parental leave. Experience of a dismissal case that had gone to an Employment Tribunal had entailed some costs in defending the case, but it had led to the introduction of a new procedure which was admitted to entail only minimal managerial time while also, in the words of one partner, making 'us more professional'.

In this way, a tribunal for wrongful dismissal can be seen as not simply a problem for the firm but, in actuality, a productive process identifying problems within the organisation and its practices.

The complex effects of regulation are further heightened because owner-managers' understanding is often vague on the details (Marlow, 2003; Hart and Blackburn, 2005). For example, while they express *general* dissatisfaction with regulatory conditions, relatively few report being affected by *specific* provisions (Atkinson and Curtis, 2004; Carter *et al.*, 2009). Particular regulations, and how they are interpreted, will affect businesses in different ways owing to differences in firm size, age and sector (Arrowsmith *et al.*, 2003; Hart and Blackburn, 2005;

Morris *et al.*, 2005), as well as to competitive conditions, degrees of regulatory enforcement and the responses of others in the firm's external and internal environments (Harris, 2000; Kitching, 2006). This creates a range of particular understandings of how a given set of regulations may apply to an organisation with owner-manager understanding often negotiated, drawing on a variety of sources such as external advisers, customers and employees (Kitching, 2006).

While much is, rightly, made of employer ignorance concerning specific regulatory provisions, it is important to highlight Edwards *et al.*'s (2004) observation that employees also have a role to play in how employment rights are enacted within a given business. As we have seen, the employment relationship is negotiated between owner-managers and employees and this will impact upon the effects of regulation. For example, in Atkinson *et al.* (2014), we discuss how employees across a variety of businesses lacked much in the way of knowledge concerning their employment rights. Consequently, owner-managers tended not to be judged in terms of regulatory compliance but more by perceptions of 'fairness' against the terms they themselves had legitimised, through formal documents such as employment handbooks, health and safety guidelines or redundancy selection criteria. Even where employees felt aggrieved by management decisions, explicit action was not taken. This is problematic since owner-managers, regardless of their integrity or intent, are not the best people to exclusively define employee understandings of their rights and obligations.

The negotiated nature of employment relationships in SMEs, combined with ignorance among both employers and employees, help to explain why employment regulation seems to have less of an impact than much of the politics surrounding this topic would have us believe. The tone of this debate matters because if ill-informed opinions are discussed over research-driven empirical findings, subsequent actions informed by the debate may prove unhelpful. Again, a focus on practices within SMEs is necessary to understand fully people management in these firms. In conclusion, we therefore agree with Carter *et al.* (2009: 276), who suggest that:

> regulation has attracted more attention than is justified by its significance. It is, of course, important that governments should be encouraged to produce better regulation (Bannock, 2006). However, the evidence presented [in their study] suggests that it would be more productive if the debate on how to create a thriving enterprise economy shifted to issues that genuinely impinge on the vitality of the small business sector.

## Conclusion

In this chapter we have considered the topic of staff turnover and used this to facilitate discussing a topic of more general concern in the employment relationships and practices of SMEs – namely, regulation. Our discussion of staff turnover found that it may be best thought of as neither simply bad nor good, but rather as depending on a number of considerations. We have suggested, therefore, that staff turnover can have different implications for firms, and draw different responses, owing to the type and position of the business concerned. Such a conclusion may appear somewhat common sense or obvious, which is why it remains interesting to find frequently polarised views of regulation which are often focused on issues of staff turnover.

If political debates and general opinion surveys of owner-managers are to be believed, regulation has only one impact on SMEs and it is a negative one. Peer-reviewed and rigorously researched academic studies have indicated, on the other hand, that discussing *the impact* of regulation is akin to discussing *the impact* of staff turnover. Of course, impacts and responses vary among firms and over time, which is why, as serious students of employment relationships and practices in SMEs, it is important for us to look beyond popular representations of regulation and towards evidence and ways of understanding the details of practice. Inevitably, this approach encounters greater complexity and, perhaps, more ambiguity when working towards conclusions, but we suggest that the effort is justified by reaching better-informed conclusions.

# Part III
# Rethinking HRM in SMEs

# 8 SME growth, HRM and the role of formalisation

In this chapter we develop our discussion around the dynamic interactions between formality and informality in SMEs' employment relationships and practices. We suggest that this is particularly important to understand when considering business growth. There is an acknowledgement that as businesses grow they become more formal, a process described as 'formalisation'. We will build on some of the insights into formality and informality the book has developed so far to gain a greater understanding of business growth. This chapter will therefore begin by defining the role of informality and formality in SMEs and then develop a dynamic approach to understanding business growth in relation to practices in use before broadening our discussion of informality and formality within SMEs' employment relationships and practices.

## The informality of SMEs

As our discussion of areas such as recruitment and selection, training and development and so on have demonstrated, SMEs are characterised as predominantly informal operations (Ram *et al.*, 2001). Informality has been defined, in a wide-ranging examination of the term by sociologist Barbara Misztal, as 'a form of interaction among partners enjoying relative freedom in interpretation of their roles' requirements' (Misztal, 2000: 46). Under this view of informality, notions of trust, personal interaction and shared understanding are brought to the fore, indicating how people seek to rely on others and the relationships they share for coordinating their own actions. In an organisational context this means recognising the roles played by, for example, friendship groups, casual conversations and unofficial rules in governing the operation of the enterprise.

SMEs, and small firms in particular, frequently exhibit close spatial and social proximity, which may foster overlap between personal and working relationships (Ram, 1999) and a greater degree of familiarity in the workplace (Goss, 1991). The close proximity underpinning these relationships can facilitate the ad hoc 'mutual coordination' of flexible tasks and roles associated with SMEs as they seek to cope with the demands posed by their internal and external environments (Misztal, 2000: 132; for discussions of Misztal's work in relation to SMEs, see Marlow *et al.*, 2010, and Mallett and Wapshott, 2014). Much of the working context associated with SMEs can therefore be understood in terms of informality.

Completing work tasks on ad hoc, informal bases, according to internal and external negotiations and perceived business needs, allows routines to evolve over time to address various organisational challenges (Scott *et al.*, 1989; Ram *et al.*, 2001; Beaver and Prince, 2004; Taylor, 2005). These routines, shaped through informal negotiations of mutually adjusted working relationships, still reflect the complex interplay of power and conflict of competing and shared interests within the organisation (Edwards, 1986; Adler, 1995; Taylor *et al.*, 2002; Wapshott and Mallett, 2013). A relative absence of codified, formal and inflexible organisational structures can mean that these interactions give rise to subtle and rapid adjustments between parties as they continually gauge their position relative to others in the firm and its wider operating context.

This predominantly informal approach to employment relationships and practices can suit SMEs, especially small firms, but as these organisations grow, they often display signs of increased formality (Kotey and Sheridan, 2004). However, the processes of organisation growth, and the place of increased formality associated with it, are problematic and cannot be assumed to resemble a transition from one (informal) state to another (formal) state (Ram and Edwards, 2010; Mallett and Wapshott, 2014).

## Inevitable formalisation with growth?

While predominantly informal, employment relationships in SMEs also feature degrees of formality (Perrow, 1970; Ram *et al.*, 2001). Even for very small businesses, activities such as employing staff can introduce degrees of formality, for example as considerations of health and safety or employment regulations become more relevant (Martin *et al.*, 2004; Jordan *et al.*, 2013). Formality can be understood as 'the presence, recognition, and consistent and appropriate use of dedicated written policies and procedures within key areas of the employment relationship' (Marlow *et al.*, 2010: 957). You will note from this definition that Marlow *et al.* focus not only on the *existence* of policies but, crucially, also include consideration of whether and how these policies *relate to practice*.

### Growth and formalisation

Within the study of entrepreneurship and SMEs generally, there is a tendency to focus on business growth. As Storey observes:

> although decline and closure are by a considerable margin the most likely outcomes over time for new and small firms, the vast bulk of theorizing and empirical work on the topic has chosen to focus on the tiny proportion of enterprises that grow.
>
> (Storey, 2011: 316)

The motivation behind the focus on growth in SME research is nicely summed up by Levie and Lichtenstein (2010: 317), when they write that 'new businesses that grow are seen as rare and valuable and therefore, are worthy of study'. We might add that the study of SME growth remains politically attractive and, perhaps, researchers are more interested in what they see as dynamic, politically relevant growth firms rather than those in decline. For example, UK Prime Minister David Cameron, in a 2014 speech reporting on progress in his government's attempts to reduce regulation, remarked that this would:

> make it easier for you to grow, to create jobs and to help give this country the long-term security we are working towards. More than 1.3 million new jobs have been created since I came to office – many of them by small businesses. And I know many of you want to grow further – or may be thinking of employing your first person – but have been put off or held back by red tape.
>
> (Cameron, 2014)

Perhaps as a result of these potential benefits, SME growth has received, and continues to receive, a great deal of attention from researchers seeking to explain it definitively. Levie and Lichtenstein identify and critique over 100 business growth models where researchers have sought to identify stages of growth along with the attendant problems facing firms growing from start-up to more established enterprise. The search for a general pattern of growth underlying these models perhaps reflects a belief that once the process of growth can be mapped, it becomes possible to replicate it or target interventions at particular stages.

From analysing these stages models of business growth, Levie and Lichtenstein (2010: 319) distil three underlying propositions:

1. In growing enterprises, distinctive stages of organisation development can be identified.
2. Organisations pass through a common sequence of stages (and therefore follow a predictable path).
3. As they develop, organisations progress towards a common end point.

Reflecting on what these underlying propositions might mean for employment relationships and practices in SMEs, we can consider that if organisations pass through common stages towards a common end point, it might be assumed that shifts from informality to formality constitute a part of this progress and are similarly predictable. This perspective makes an intuitive kind of sense: smaller firms tend to be informal and large firms have greater degrees of formality. Formalising might therefore be associated with a number of necessary adjustments organisations are required to make as they grow.

As we discussed in Chapter 2, as organisations grow in scale the opportunities for personal oversight by an owner-manager can be reduced. In a small organisation, characterised by close spatial and social proximity, an owner-manager might work alongside employees either in a role akin to a co-worker or perhaps simply through a lack of space. This kind of co-location offers opportunities for owner-managers to oversee and provide direction to employees directly, in ways that may not always be to employees' liking (Goss, 1991). Nevertheless, as an organisation grows, the possibility for an owner-manager to see everything that goes on and know everyone in the business can be diminished.

If standardised ways of working are introduced, for instance in the form of standard operating procedures, then the need for personal oversight may be reduced as the formal system provides the necessary direction. Introducing some standardised ways of working and means of channelling information back to management enables decisions to be made about the business and directions given as to what tasks are required for completion. Likewise, as new staff join a business there are procedures for them to follow that enable their contribution to fit into the existing ways of working, as opposed to the organisation having to adjust to accommodate multiple, idiosyncratic approaches to the same task (Perrow, 1970; Stinchcombe, 2001).

However, in testing the underlying assumptions and the broader validity of over 100 stages and life-cycle models of firm growth, Levie and Lichtenstein conclude that they are without empirical basis. Levie and Lichtenstein do identify support for the idea that growing businesses exhibit distinguishable stages at different times but conclude that there is no consensus on the number or inter-relation of these stages. Further, and of key importance, they argue that there is no empirical support for the idea that all businesses follow the same sequence of stages as they grow.

So, beyond general operational considerations of coping with larger organisations, the fact of business growth and accompanying changes tells us little of *how* SMEs might increase degrees of formality as they grow, particularly regarding employment relationships and practices. It is to these more detailed challenges at the level of the enterprise that we can now turn, to explain why seeking to effectively embed greater degrees of formality is neither simple nor straightforward (Gilman and Edwards, 2008; Edwards and Ram, 2010).

## Making the 'right' changes

Standardising ways of working, whether this is in terms of new practices or choosing certain existing ways of working above others, involves identifying a 'best way' of doing something. Adopting formal policies or practices to control what was previously accomplished through informal, interpersonal means can impact employment relationships as well as the practices in question. Practices that were once open to negotiation and mutual adjustment (Ram, 1999; Wapshott and Mallett, 2013) become codified and increasingly rigid, reducing reliance on shared understandings and trust, jarring existing relationships (Misztal, 2000; Mallett and Wapshott, 2014). This observation underlines the distinction between policy and practice that we will discuss again in Chapter 9.

Acknowledging the need for change and adaptation as organisations grow, as suggested by growth models and associated work, does not mean that the changes implemented are necessarily effective or that the 'right' changes are apparent. Thinking about which formal policies are introduced, and how, helps to illustrate this point. According to Phelps *et al.* (2007) in their conceptual paper 'Life cycles of growing organizations: a review with implications for knowledge and learning', an increase in formality can be a rational response to the operational problems businesses encounter as they grow. Phelps and his colleagues suggest that organisations will implement changes in different areas of the business as required and such an approach can appear potentially ad hoc, creating a kind of patchwork formality in organisations. In organisations we have studied this has tended to lead to some aspects of employment relationships being covered by formal practices, more- or less-implemented, while other aspects were left alone.

This patchwork, ad hoc feel may also be reflected in the policies themselves, imported from clients or former employers. Rather than strategic responses to specific challenges, policies developed originally in very different contexts can be grafted onto the organisation with little thought as to whether or not the policy will achieve the desired purpose. This policy patchwork is something we have encountered to varying degrees in the businesses we have studied. As the operations manager of a financial services industry recruitment firm explained when discussing where certain formal policies had come from:

> I'll be totally honest, I'm not sure because [the formal HR policies] were in place when I got here ... I think a lot of the things, that maybe we've put in place, you do crib off, because everybody does ... we all crib off each other really but where he [the owner] actually got that from I don't know.

At both a communications consultancy and a science-based recruitment firm, policies still occasionally bore the branding or terminology of the 'donor' organisation, while at a specialist publishing business, the new 'values framework' closely resembled structures developed at the HR and Operations Managers' respective, very large, former employers. Thus, the decision to implement greater degrees of formality in the firms appeared ad hoc and, at times, ill-fitted to the business' operational capacity and needs. This is in contrast to suggestions that formal policies and processes are introduced to meet specific operational demands.

Perhaps such behaviours and outcomes are to be expected. If owner managers are unaccustomed to many of the formal policies and systems available for managing the employment relationship, they might have limited knowledge of what will work in their organisation. Even if they have prior experience in other businesses, the systems in place there might not suit their own, possibly smaller enterprise. Limited knowledge or experience of formal management tools, combined with the demands of running a business, may help explain why some SMEs seek to copy what they see working elsewhere, without tailoring it specifically to the needs of their own business, which could be quite different.

## Formalisation that is not growth

As already noted, business growth is a widely researched, debated and promoted topic. In an interesting and provocative article on business growth and performance, Kiviluoto (2013: 572) suggests that:

> Growth is something that has come to achieve a myth-like status. It is admired, widely discussed and entrepreneurs achieving growth are portrayed as heroes.

However, as Kiviluoto argues, business growth is not part of the everyday realities of running an SME for many owner-managers. On the contrary, the majority of firms do not grow in size but are, for roughly half of all new businesses, likely to fail within the first four years (Storey, 2011). Work by Alex Coad and colleagues (2013) highlighted this by tracking a profile of 6,247 new businesses over a period of six years. After the first year, 5,192 businesses had survived, with median sales of £39,276 (note: these are sales, not profits!). Five years later, two-thirds of the firms were no longer trading, and while median sales for the survivors had increased, this was not a dramatic increase and stood at £48,775 (for the purposes of the study, median sales figures were not adjusted for inflation). These findings highlighted that only a small proportion of the firms demonstrated significant and consistent sales growth over the period (Coad et al., 2013). However, a large amount of research continues to focus on high-growth businesses, ignoring the everyday working experiences of most SMEs.

This has important implications for our understanding of informality, formality and processes of formalisation in SMEs. Not only is significant business growth uncommon, but it is also not the only driver of attempts to increase degrees of formality. To understand increased formality in the employment relationships and practices of small businesses, we need to acknowledge the role of non-operational considerations that may prompt the implementation of particular policies or changes in the day-to-day working relationships. For example, SMEs have been found to implement formal policies to satisfy the real or perceived demands of external stakeholders, such as clients or regulatory bodies (Ram, 2000), meaning that a formal policy is not always supported by complementary practices.

In such instances formal policy can be an 'empty shell' (Hoque and Noon, 2004), drawing a veil between the external stakeholders who desire formality and the internal operations of the firm that continue on a largely informal basis – a façade that employers and employees (and, at times, even academics!) collude in maintaining (Marlow et al., 2010). At the scientific recruitment firm, the owner-manager seemed driven by a personal desire for the enterprise to be seen by outsiders as 'legitimate'. To this end, he had adopted a range of sophisticated formal policies relating to all aspects of people management in the firm. Its Investors in People (IiP) accreditation, discussed in Chapter 5, was one signal of the business' sophistication and alluded to the owner-manager's quest for legitimation:

> It's not just a logo that you put on your paper or a plaque you put on your wall. Clients do recognise that, you know. 'Yes you are a small business but you do have professional standards, you are going for Investors in People, you are doing this, so, you know, you're just a smaller version of some of the bigger boys'.

This owner-manager expresses the value of IiP, and its associated formal policies, in terms of signalling to clients and not in terms of responding to growth or improving business processes. Studying this firm, it soon became apparent that the practical weight of sustaining application of many of these formalities was too great for the organisation. Policies fell from practice as the owner-manager focused on the day-to-day running of the business. As a result, some staff became cynical of such initiatives, however much they acknowledged the good intentions behind their introduction.

We have also found this 'empty shell' formality deployed *within* businesses, for example at TechCo where the use of redundancy criteria masked informal decisions over which employees were targeted for redundancy (discussed in Chapter 7; see Atkinson *et al.*, 2014 for more detail). Similarly, at an IT-based business, interviews with the administration team discussed how, each year, the top-ranked performers across the business were put into a bonus pool. In departments with quantifiable targets for sales or customer satisfaction, the scoring system is relatively straightforward. However, it was less clear how this could work for the administration team, an internal service department. An administrator said:

> I had it [the scoring system] on an email one time but it is not put anywhere. Like our other golden rules are always in [the company newsletter] that comes out every month. But these ones, no, I can't remember, it is obviously a lot to do with attitude and, do you know, I can't remember.

The scoring criteria were outlined in the company newsletter which featured league tables and included the formal scoring system for the administration team (though for no other teams). This included criteria such as 'be on time', 'keep work area tidy', 'attend and contribute to meetings', 'show commitment to the team' and 'share our work ethic', among others. Perhaps surprisingly, given the vagueness of the scoring criteria, the staff all had very similar scores, often with only one or two points between them, as if suggesting some precision in the scoring. We began to wonder more about the scoring system when employees explained the reasons for their narrowly missing out on the bonus pool:

> Well for that particular thing, because I was so demotivated thinking is it just because ... and [manager] did feed it back. It is awkward because I am sort of friends with [manager] as well. But she did just say it was one of those things and you missed out by this much [indicating a tiny amount]. And I actually put a note on my schedule every Tuesday and Thursday to remind myself just to make a conscious effort to set that bit of an example and not be too ... you know, just make a conscious effort not to chat across the office or do something like that. Because I didn't really know what else to do apart from ... and she even said there is nothing else to feed back ... I think it was just the whole ... a bit more growing up.

It seemed as though too much talking or chatting was a fairly common (and rather thin) reason offered by way of feedback to staff who had not made it into the bonus pool. When we explored with managers precisely how the scoring system was applied for administrators, they admitted that a rather less formal arrangement was in place. In practice, the managers held a meeting at the end of the year in which they would share their overall opinions on who they thought should go into the bonus pool. In turn, this required managers to devise explanations as to why particular individuals had missed out:

> I think we need to put something in place to make [scoring] as open and as fair as possible. Because next Friday I am going to have to deal with the aftermath of the people who think they deserved a place and could have deserved a place. And there are people that will come to me and say, 'Right, okay, I didn't get in, what do I have to do to get in next year?' But because it is not scored and it is not ... it is really difficult to answer that question. So this year's choices have been made by [managers] getting into a room and arguing it out. And one of the girls who I know is expecting it this year hasn't got in ... and she is the kind of person who will come and say, 'Okay, why haven't I got in?' So [senior manager] went through the conversation. And it just so happens that [manager] was backing her to get into the bonus pool but, obviously, with four managers in a room, it ended up being someone else. So I have got like a list of things to say ready.

In this business, staff accepted the management decisions as they were presented, as the outcome of applying a formal management policy. In each company, however, the formal policy was only a veneer of formality obscuring the informal application of management discretion. The use of formality in this way appeared to grant some legitimacy to what were potentially divisive decisions. Outcomes that appear to result from an objective, formal policy that has been carefully applied may be more palatable to those affected than the practice-in-use of managers making a decision informally and then presenting it in formal tones.

The ad hoc use of different degrees of (in)formality in response to particular internal and external demands indicates that informality and formality can be considered co-existent (Marlow et al., 2010). Instead of a competing duality, this co-existence can therefore be understood in a more dynamic way, attentive to the complexities and messiness of practices in use and some of the tensions between control and autonomy. Focusing attention too much on the challenges of business growth risks simplifying the introduction and development of formal policies and practices in SMEs.

## Formalising relationships

Even when firms increase degrees of formality, degrees of informality often persist in their day-to-day operations. Owner-managers commonly prefer forms of personal supervision and may seek to informally defend their authority as they replace unwritten understandings with more formalised practices (Nadin and Cassell, 2007; Marlow et al., 2010), attempting to formalise some areas of the business but not others. Such areas might include policies around HR, operations and compliance, but also working practices themselves can become formalised (for example, through standard operating procedures), as can the employment relationship and general tone of communication and interaction within the firm (Mallett and Wapshott, 2014).

In our work with SMEs, managers typically expressed a desire to retain an informal 'feel' in the organisations even as they sought to formalise aspects of the employment relationship. This concern with retaining degrees of informality seemed particularly pronounced in firms where senior management attached importance to retaining a sense of close social relations within the organisation. Christian, who, as managing director of 130 employees at the IT-based company, continued to conduct a daily walk-about at the head office, explained:

> I know everybody's wife or husband or partner's name ... and I think that is really, really important. Because you can't be interested in half of a unit can you? No, I think that's ... no, I think that is absolutely important.

This was bolstered by members of the company's senior management team taking turns in working from branch offices on a regular basis to maintain links between management and staff across the organisation. In other businesses, owners and managers shared open-plan workspaces with employees or could otherwise be found out of their offices and chatting casually with employees. A founder and director at the communications company we studied explained:

> There is an issue around respect and I think entrepreneurs behave in different ways. What we've done here is, there's definitely an entrepreneurial spirit, my approach has always been to make sure that we develop people by sitting alongside them and working with them and having a laugh and a joke with them and make the place an enjoyable place to work. I don't want that to change but I think the structure of the organisation now, the

types of business that we do, means that there's got to be an element of separation because you can't be all things to all people.

This sense of maturity in the business on the part of owner-managers can sometimes drive a desire for greater formality in employment relationships. So, for example, in this organisation, the company directors moved themselves to a separate floor from their employers, no longer mingling as co-workers and now expecting to be addressed in more formal terms. As the business changes the ways in which owner-managers view themselves and expect to be treated impacts, in turn, on employees and their relationship with their employers and with the business more generally. We have found that it can be difficult for employees to make this adjustment. Where they have been with a firm for a significant part of its history, maybe from start-up, and have become used to close social and spatial proximity with the owner-managers, they can become deeply invested in the business and its aims. To be suddenly treated as hired hands can be an unsettling shock.

In this way, owner-managers can struggle to maintain a balance between the informality they associate with the 'small firm feel' of the organisation's past and the formality that is viewed as necessary for the business to run on more 'professional' lines. The tensions between the flexibility allowed by informality and the professionalism associated with formality, in the firms we have worked with, are often perceived not only in policies and practices but the tone and forms of interaction that take place on an everyday basis. Degrees of formality and informality can co-exist in unproblematic ways, but they can also contradict and undermine each other, creating confusion and a sense of ambiguity, uncertainty and even mistrust (Mallett and Wapshott, 2014).

## Persistence and co-existence of informality

Many firms do not grow and the realities of everyday business for many firms is one of struggle and, often, failure. The challenges faced in maintaining a successful business need not, therefore, always be considered in terms of business growth and related to operational changes (Kiviluoto, 2013). Further, as we have argued throughout the book, a simple 'from–to' approach to understanding SMEs over time, for example in relation to formalisation or in the transition from entrepreneur to owner-manager, can be limited and, in many ways, unhelpful (Watson, 1995). This kind of thinking can be found in many aspects of the world around us and, in his work on informal economic activities, Colin Williams (2007), for example, in his book *Rethinking the future of work*, explains the underlying mechanics of the approach very clearly and in detail (so you may wish to follow this up in your own wider reading).

For our current purposes we can set out some particular problems in conceiving of a relatively straightforward, linear development from informality to formality. Our central concern is to recognise how informality and formality co-exist in organisations and how, even in those that display increasing tendencies towards more formal ways of working, informality persists. As noted already in Chapter 4, it is an error simply to associate SMEs with informality and large firms with a formal approach. In fact, as highlighted by Monder Ram and his colleagues (2001) and by Arthur L. Stinchcombe (2001), all organisations require degrees of informality and formality to operate. In terms of the balance between informality and formality in SMEs and large organisations, the difference is 'a matter of degree and not kind, and its nature may vary as much between firms of a given size as between large and small ones' (Ram et al., 2001: 846). This means that representations of SMEs that imply a move from informal to formal ways of working or interacting in the workplace risk fundamentally misrepresenting how organisations function. If there is a change that occurs, it is in the balance, and associated tensions, between informality and formality.

A second problem with understanding organisations as moving from informality to formal ways of working is that it underplays the distinctions between policies and practices. Reflect on some of the examples earlier in this chapter or your own experience of work and you are likely to recognise that having a formal policy in place is not the same thing as that policy being implemented. For example, there may be a policy that forbids the use of mobile phones in a library or train carriage. This does not necessarily mean that phones will not be used. If you are new to this environment and see other people using their phones without sanction then, over time, you may learn the unwritten rules that suggest circumstances in which mobile phones can be used. The practices in use differ from the policies in place, and to understand how the library or carriage works, one must observe these practices in use. Routines may develop over time such that there are unspoken rules that exist independently of formal policies. Often, organisations are too 'messy' for us to identify if the existence of a formal policy means that we can be sure day-to-day practices will comply or if, for example, our focus on this formal policy obscures informally negotiated routines that have developed in its place.

These informal routines suggest a final problem we can identify with treating informality and formality as distinct ways of operating: a tendency to overplay the differences between these characterisations in practice. These informal routines can become embedded in practice to the point where they are effectively indistinguishable from formal practices. Further, as you have seen already in this chapter, and elsewhere in the book, managers can use rather informal means, albeit presented under a formal veneer, to achieve particular objectives. Moreover, Marlow et al. (2010: 961) describe how an 'oscillation between formal and informal [practices at a business they studied meant that employees] felt there was little point in raising grievances formally as little would be done and that established social networks persisted if they wanted to circumvent formal systems'.

In order to address these problems, we need to accept that informality and formality co-exist in organisations. The particular interaction of informality and formality might shift over time and where the organisation encounters different sets of circumstances, both externally and internally (Levie and Lichtenstein,

2010). Some of the changes might be driven by practical considerations associated with enterprise growth, but also by a range of other considerations that help to shape employment relationships and practices (Harney and Dundon, 2006; Gilman and Edwards, 2008).

However real these pressures can be, it is nevertheless important to remember that informality and formality co-exist in employment relationships and practices. Establishing more formal relationships and practices does not exclude a role for informality. By viewing organisations as exhibiting degrees of formality–informality, where informality and formality co-exist and are co-dependent, any dichotomous, restricting decision to pursue either informality or formality becomes redundant. What matters is how informality and formality interact in the employment relationship (Mallett and Wapshott, 2014), and what works for a given organisation at a given time. In this way we can understand that even in growing SMEs, informality will remain a persistent element of how organisations function, including their employment relationships and practices.

### Task 8.1

As small firms grow and take on additional staff it is often suggested that they become more formal in terms of employment policies and relationships. What do you think happens to the degrees of informality/formality when businesses shed employees and reduce in size?

## Conclusion

This chapter has discussed SME growth in relation to a key area of employment relationships and practices: formalisation. While a large amount of research literature has sought to describe business growth in predictable, life-cycle models, we have drawn on an alternative, critical literature to suggest that this risks over-simplifying the messy practicalities of organisation life. The life-cycle approach tells us little of *how* SMEs might increase degrees of formality as they grow or seek to satisfy other motivations.

From this perspective we can understand the limitations and dangers of viewing formalisation as a relatively straightforward, rational operational response to growth or changes in an enterprise's environment. Instead, formalisation can perform a range of functions beyond operational changes demanded by growth – for example, providing a veil across informal practices for both external and internal audiences.

Engaging with the details found at the level of organisations' practices, rather than broad overviews of policies alone, we have identified how formalising organisational practices and relationships represent challenges for SMEs. It can often be difficult for owner-managers to know how to increase formality in terms of policies and practices and there seems to be a persistent dilemma over whether or not to increase the degrees of formality in the working relationships in the business. From an employee perspective, attempts to alter the dynamics of day-to-day interactions in the workplace can be disruptive and introduce uncertainty to existing relationships.

It is important, in understanding the roles of informality and formality in organisations, to recognise their *co-existence*; this is true for large as well as small organisations. What matters is how this co-existence plays out, the balance between these co-existing and, at times, contradictory elements of organisational life. Consequently, we have questioned representations of SMEs moving *from* one state *to* another in terms of informality and formality. Rather, the challenge lies in understanding how to accommodate the tensions, and recognise the benefits, of informality and formality co-existing in organisations.

# 9 Employment relationships and practices in SMEs

In the book so far we have sought to explore and understand employment relationships and practices in SMEs on their own terms. Typically, this has been with a view to considering whether firms' practices make sense in their given contexts. A relatively recent concern in the literature on SMEs has been to discover whether the ways in which firms manage employment relationships and practices can be shown to impact on organisation performance. This body of research, developed over the past 25 years or so in the mainstream HRM literature, has been applied increasingly to SMEs via 'high performance work systems' (HPWS). In this chapter we will discuss and critique this recent development in terms of how it may shape understanding of employment relationships and practices in SMEs. We do this by discussing a selection of the key studies and concepts, the insights they provide but also, by drawing on the ideas we have raised so far in the book and our emphasis on employment relationships and practices, where there may be limitations or difficulties with this research agenda.

## High performance work systems

While we have so far looked at particular practices such as recruitment or training and development separately, a currently popular way of considering HRM policies and practices generally, and increasingly in relation to SMEs, is to consider them as strategic packages or bundles of practices. This approach suggests that it is necessary to understand how the practices work together. Such strategic packages of management practices, aimed at maximising performance, can be understood as high performance work systems (also referred to in the literature as 'high performance work practices' and 'high commitment management') and, in an early attempt to explore them in relation to SMEs, they have been defined as:

> a set of distinctive but interrelated HRM practices that together select, develop, retain, and motivate a workforce: (1) that possess superior abilities (i.e., superior (a broad repertoire of) skills and behavior scripts); (2) that applies their abilities in the work-related activities; (3) whose work-related

activities (i.e., actual employee behaviors/output) result in these firms achieving superior immediate indicators of firm performance (i.e., those indicators over which the workforce has direct control) and sustainable competitive advantage.

(Way, 2002: 765–6)

Studies of HPWS have tended to draw upon the resource-based view (RBV) of the firm, most commonly associated with Jay Barney (1991) but with roots at least as far back as Edith Penrose's (1959) book *The Theory of the Growth of the Firm*. The RBV holds that resources internal to a firm may provide a basis for sustainable competitive advantage. It gained traction in studies of HRM (see Wright et al., 1994) as a means of conceptually linking employees and business performance outcomes, an association that was intuitively attractive but underdeveloped theoretically and empirically. Way (2002) argues that small businesses tend to be more labour intensive than large businesses and that they have limited alternative sources of competitive advantage (also see Greer et al., 2015). A focus on maximising the internal 'human resources' and understanding how employees and performance may be linked has therefore been viewed as offering significant potential gains for small businesses.

Despite the attractions of HPWS and early signs of success in discovering performance links (for example Huselid, 1995), the field in general has been subject to criticisms and limitations. Before we discuss the application of this approach to SMEs, it is therefore worth briefly outlining some of these limitations. At a conceptual level, Frank Mueller (1996) argued that separating out human resources from other aspects of an organisation that contribute to performance is unhelpful when trying to understand overall organisation performance, resulting in 'a sterile debate about which [assets] are analytically prior or more important' (ibid.: 776; Purcell, 1999). Instead, Mueller argues, one group of company 'assets' must be understood in terms of its interdependence with other company assets.

Moreover, while 'high performance work system' is a widely used label that can appear to represent a stable concept and collection of practices, little such commonality exists across studies. In an early demonstration of this variety, Dyer and Reeves (1995) highlighted that across four major studies, 28 HR policies and practices were measured with 'formal training' being the only common feature and very little commonality elsewhere between the studies.

Beyond the diverse policies and practices being considered, assessments of 'performance' have also been questioned. Paauwe and Boselie (2005) indicate that 'performance' can mean financial outcomes, organisational outcomes, HR-related outcomes or combinations of outcomes to create more general performance measures. Although diversity of practices studied and measures adopted is to be expected, it does mean that studies in this area need to be examined carefully before they can be compiled into a single body of research evidence.

The challenges identified in the 1990s and first decade of this century have yet to be resolved adequately, with Delmotte et al. (2012: 1481) recently suggesting that 'to date, we know little about the conditions under which HR practices are (not) effective'. Sentiments that are echoed by David E. Guest, in his must-read review of HPWS research, 'Human resource management and performance: still searching for some answers', in which he concludes that 'after hundreds of research studies we are still in no position to assert with any confidence that good HRM has an impact on organisation performance' (Guest, 2011: 11).

## High performance work systems in SMEs

In the search for maximised performance, a range of studies has been published with somewhat mixed findings. One of the first studies to look in detail at HPWS in SMEs was Sean A. Way's (2002) paper 'High performance work systems and intermediate indicators of firm performance within the US small business sector'. Way studied firms ranging from 20 to 99 employees, using the National Employer Survey to test hypotheses that HPWS decrease staff turnover and increase productivity. He found evidence for a decrease in staff turnover and for increased productivity, as perceived by the owner-managers, but not when assessed in terms of an external measure of overall labour productivity. Importantly, for Way, this means that the outcomes produced through the adoption of HPWS did not necessarily exceed the labour costs required by the systems themselves.

In a pair of papers, Luc Sels and colleagues (2006a, 2006b) sought to understand where the links between HRM and performance could be generalised to small businesses. They surveyed 416 Belgian firms ranged between ten and 100 employees, asking owner-managers to complete the survey as well as drawing on financial data for each firm. They found that the intensity of engagement with HRM practices, in areas such as training and development and performance management, had a strong effect on firm productivity which impacted positively on the personnel costs and value added to the business. Interestingly, this effect was not sufficient compensation for the increased costs associated with achieving this degree of intensity. Such costs include, for example, direct costs such as the salary for an HR manager or obtaining HR systems. However, there are also indirect costs, for example through the costs incurred in the loss to productivity of an employee leaving the business to engage in formal training. In the case of increased employee voice, often an important part of HPWS, this involves time out for everyone, including the owner-manager. There are also potentially negative impacts from work intensification or other problems (e.g. feeling disengaged from business) which can damage productivity and lead to higher absenteeism.

The work of Sels and colleagues therefore lends some support to Way (2002), suggesting potential limitations to the value of these types of HRM or HPWS for SMEs. However, when measuring the total effect of HRM intensity on *profitability*, Sels *et al.* found that this *did* exceed the costs and they therefore assumed that:

This effect can be explained by the positive impact of HRM intensity on some nonmeasured operational performance outcomes such as a lower level of disputes, better quality and/or more innovation.

(Sels *et al.*, 2006b: 96)

Clearly, HPWS are part of broader organisational processes and performance will be shaped by a range of interacting, direct and indirect influences. Messersmith and Wales (2013) set out to explore some of this complexity in their study of 119 young high-tech firms, examining the fit between the entrepreneurial orientation of the business and its strategic approach to HRM, specifically in terms of HPWS and what the paper terms a philosophy of partnership in the employer's attitudes to employees. Messersmith and Wales found that the firm's entrepreneurial orientation impacted performance where HPWS and a partnership philosophy were also present. That is, their findings suggest that businesses need these systems in place to make the most of their employees in delivering the benefits of an entrepreneurial orientation.

These studies provide interesting insights into the questions surrounding HRM and performance, but it is important to read them in detail to appreciate fully both their value and their potential limitations. To understand in more depth what these types of studies are looking at and their relevance to our understanding of managing human resources in SMEs, we will therefore consider a particular study in detail. To do this we have chosen to discuss a paper titled 'Human resource management and performance: evidence from small and medium-sized firms', by Maura Sheehan (2014). We have chosen this paper because it is very recent, it was published in a highly reputable, peer-reviewed journal (the *International Small Business Journal*) and, understandably given its high quality and rigour, it has been a very popular article (the most read in the journal for several months in 2014–15). Sheehan also outlines the value of her findings in terms of their practical implications for businesses and so is not presenting a purely academic exercise. The article therefore represents the 'state of the art' in this area and is a useful way of discussing both the strengths and potential limitations of this approach to SMEs and their practices.

Sheehan (2014) suggests that, owing to their external environment (e.g. increased employment regulations), SMEs are more formal than generally assumed. For example, where firms have had to comply with regulations around minimum wage or working hours, they will have had to introduce formal policies and practices to manage this compliance successfully (although see Chapter 7 on why this might not be straightforward). Sheehan is therefore interested in the impact of these formal HRM systems on performance, specifically in relation to profitability, innovation and labour turnover. These indicators of performance were measured through owner-manager self-reports of their perceived performance relative to competitors, although Sheehan used external validation for these perceptions where possible (e.g. financial information). The 1,589 firms studied had all operated for over 18 months and had between ten and 249 employees.

Importantly, Sheehan's research seeks to determine a causal relationship (the performance is a result of the HRM practices) rather than simply identifying a correlation between firms with HRM and high performance. She does this by taking measurements at two points (2007 and 2011) and controlling for past performance when assessing the impacts of HRM on present performance (see also Sels *et al.*, 2006a). The number of firms for which this was possible – that is, those which participated in both surveys – was 336.

Sheehan found a relationship between HRM and performance and confirmed that this relationship is causal. While suggesting the importance of bundles of practices (as in HPWS), Sheehan was also able to identify specific practices that related to the specific performance measures:

1. Financial performance: compensation, training and development, strategic people management.
2. Innovation: training and development, strategic people management.
3. Labour turnover: recruitment and selection, performance appraisal, employee voice/consultation, information sharing, training and development, strategic people management.

Based on these findings, Sheehan (2014: 563) draws out practical implications, suggesting the importance for SMEs in attending to the finding that 'a greater investment in the selected human resource practices has a positive effect on subsequent performance'. She emphasises the significance of these findings, in particular, for owner-managers, and they might suggest a need for any SME owner-manager reading the article to invest immediately in such policies and practices. However, it is important to remember not only the cautionary findings about the potential costs of such systems (e.g. Way, 2002), but also some of what we have learnt about SMEs in this book.

### Contesting HPWS in SMEs

Thinking about these studies in terms of what we have discussed throughout this book, several potential problems emerge: assessing the presence and impacts of HRM; employee experiences; informality; and the persistence of a deficit model.

#### Assessing the presence and impacts of HRM

Even in interesting and valuable work such as that by Messersmith and Wales (2013), there remain several potential issues that relate to the measurements involved in creating numerical representations of firms' practices and outcomes to facilitate statistical tests for relationships. Inevitably, through the standardisation necessary to perform such tests and the reduction of messy, complicated practices to testable hypotheses, some aspects of what happens in SMEs are going to be lost. This is potentially exacerbated when Messersmith and Wales identify the presence of HPWS and partnership philosophy by asking owner-managers (or similar) at each firm, ignoring the views and experiences of employees (see the next section). This is not to doubt the empirical value of Messersmith and Wales's work, but rather to suggest the need for additional research to understand some of these details in greater depth.

This concern echoes a point raised by John Purcell (1999) writing in relation to HPWP research more generally. Purcell suggests that faced with a checklist or series of short questions about potentially complex aspects of an organisation, the temptation for the respondent to write down guesses rather than checking the accurate responses must be strong. Where asked about, for example, the value of seeking employee feedback, the dynamic, everyday practices within the business may be more nuanced and complicated than can be captured with a rating from one to five. However, with only one respondent per organisation, these responses have to be taken as accurate.

Importantly, while controls can be put in place for some measures, this approach puts a lot of trust in owner-managers not only to report honestly but accurately in terms of standard definitions for practices in use (Purcell, 1999; Edwards and Ram, 2010). For example, as we discussed in Chapter 5, drawing on Smith *et al.* (2002), owner-managers may not recognise certain practices, such as informal training and development, as appropriate when asked a survey question. As in Sheehan's research, where participants were given descriptions of the relevant practices beforehand, this will partly depend on the scope of the descriptions provided (in Sheehan's case, she acknowledges a focus on formal policies and practices). It is not therefore, just that owner-managers might inflate particular practices (especially if they relate to strategic or other positively value-laden concepts – see, for example, Bacon *et al.*, 1996, discussed in Chapter 5), but they may also ignore practices that are in use but remain unspoken and which are not considered within the formal language of human resource management and associated research. For example, when an owner-manager assigns a failing employee to learn from a more experienced colleague, they may not consider themselves engaged in HRM.

There is a further problem with owner-manager self-reports of HRM practices suggested by the research of Tocher and Rutherford (2009). They emphasise that, lacking in resources and busy running the business, how much attention can (or do) owner-managers actually give specifically to HRM issues? Tocher and Rutherford suggest that it is not until the issues become a significant problem that they will receive attention, echoing conceptions of SMEs as ad hoc and reactive. In their study, Tocher and Rutherford found that the owner-managers of high-performing firms were less likely to perceive acute HRM problems, although they were more likely to perceive them if they were more experienced, had a larger firm and were better educated.

> When 1,693 SME owner/managers were asked in an open-ended format to indicate the issue that was currently the most critical issue facing their

firms, 21% mentioned HRM problems. Furthermore, HRM problems were far and away the most commonly mentioned issue.

(Tocher and Rutherford, 2009: 471)

These findings suggest the limitations of survey research that asks owner-managers about HRM issues in their firms: it is not until these issues become significant problems for the business that owner-managers give them much thought or attention. Any response they give is therefore not the result of careful, balanced consideration of the practices. Moreover, if you think back to Hirschsohn's (2008) study that we outlined in Chapter 5, you will recall that, ordinarily, decisions relating to staffing are not primary concerns in organisations, perhaps especially not in SMEs. Hirschsohn argues that such matters are third- or fourth-order decisions that follow from higher priorities such as product market and operational decisions.

Returning to Sheehan's (2014) study of HRM and performance, she found that something called 'strategic people management' was particularly prominent, impacting upon all three measures of performance. It is worth considering this label and what it represents. The four practices or policies necessary to be recognised as operating strategic people management in the firms Sheehan studied were: job title denoting specialisation in employment relations/human resources; a formal strategic plan; employment relations issues covered in this plan; and Investors in People (IiP) status. Sheehan suggests that the prevalence of these practices in her UK sample is evidence 'of an ever-increasing role of more formal human resources' (ibid.: 561).

While apparently objective measures, this information (e.g. the existence of a formal plan) is reported by owner-managers. Giving this collection of self-reported statements a name like 'strategic people management', while a reasonably accurate representation of the goals of organisational plans as they relate to the employment relationship, can still risk obscuring the potentially messy practices that may be involved in these relationships on an everyday basis. Where this has important implications is in relation to one of the key themes of this book: practices in use. If we take IiP accreditation as something that can be easily verified, how much does this accreditation tell us about the practices in use within the firm? In Chapter 5 we discussed how Ram's (2000) study of IiP-accredited SMEs provides evidence that the award did little to influence the day-to-day practices. Instead, IiP was treated as a paper exercise that the businesses could use to promote themselves. In this way, whilst surface indicators such as IiP accreditation may appear to suggest formality in SMEs, the everyday practices inside the firm may be very different.

Those firms that make effective use of IiP to win contracts and impress external clients may, indeed, be higher performing than those that do not. What is often missing from studies that risk a focus on policy instead of practice, is an understanding of how the different factors measured and interrelated statistically actually produce, for example, high performance. By ignoring the practices in use and assuming that policy results in practice (Mueller, 1996), studies of HPWS in SMEs do not shine much light on *how* these systems have impacts, where these may be appropriate (or not), or in what ways they can support aspirations such as business growth.

*Employee experiences*

Given that the HRM approach generally, and HPWS more specifically, is based on the importance of 'human capital' it is perhaps surprising that many studies ignore the humans constituting this capital, treating employees as passive recipients of owner-manager HRM strategies. An interesting exception is a study by Verreynne *et al.* (2013) which analyses open-ended survey questions that collected the views of both owner-managers and employees. They found that employees' perceptions of employment systems differed in high-performing firms, where they were more likely to mention:

> flexible work practices, viable career paths, clear requirements, constructive feedback, positive feedback, positive rewards and recognition, access to training and development, a supportive culture, perception of organizational support, high involvement and good communication.
> (Verreynne *et al.*, 2013: 421)

Further, the views of employees tended to be more strategic than the views of owner-managers. Perhaps, while owner-managers are not able to give a great deal of attention to HRM issues, many of these are of greater relevance to the day-to-day experiences of employees, who are better qualified to comment on them. It is therefore worth quoting a few of the comments from Verreynne *et al.*'s paper:

> I am fully trusted by [employer]. She shows this to me by giving me certain tasks to do, allowing me to help her out. She obviously trusts my thoughts as she asks my opinion on certain things in relation to the business.
> (Verreynne *et al.*, 2013: 413)

> My pay definitely does not reflect the amount of work and time that I put into the firm. Other people in my position at other firms earn well more than I do.
> (Verreynne *et al.*, 2013: 417)

> Most of the time feedback is constructive, but sometimes it becomes emotive and causes friction between the manager and myself.
> (Verreynne *et al.*, 2013: 414)

What these comments emphasise is not just employee awareness and consideration of issues relating to HRM and HPWS, but some of the potential negatives and the complexities involved. For example, in the final quote, while an owner-manager may confidently claim that they give regular feedback, there is value in reflecting on the experience of that feedback for the employees. However, given the abbreviated nature of comments in surveys, even these responses lack the detail and complexity we might expect in everyday SME practices.

The understanding we might gain from more detailed consideration is particularly important when we want to understand how HPWS or other approaches to HRM may impact upon performance. For example, in an analysis of the 1998 Workplace Employee Relations Survey (and not focused upon SMEs), Ramsay *et al.* (2000) suggest how increased productivity may come about through intensification of work and higher insecurity, both of which are also likely to lead to job-related stress and, ultimately, problems such as high rates of absenteeism. Ramsay *et al.* also point out that employees have an important role to play in shaping organisational outcomes, something that is invariably ignored in studies of HRM, and especially HPWS, in SMEs.

*Informality*

The areas covered so far in this subsection (assessing the presence and impacts of HRM and employee experiences) relate to one of the defining elements of many SMEs: their relatively high degree of informality. As we have discussed throughout this book, informal practices are complex and messy – for example, in relation to the dynamic, direct and indirect effects of powerful external forces. These informal practices, such as the treatment of training and development, outlined in Chapter 5, can be distorted, misrepresented or simply overlooked in the survey-based methods upon which studies of HPWS have tended to rely.

However, while studies such as that by Sheehan (2014) explicitly discount informal practices, focusing instead on the formal aspects she sees as increasingly prominent, other researchers have engaged with informality and accepted that it need not be viewed negatively. Verreynne *et al.* (2013), for example, include informality in relation to practices such as flexibility. They suggest that it is the flexibility of informal practices that allows SMEs to maximise their advantage and the capabilities of their employees:

> For example, informality allowed staff to adjust tasks to suit their needs as well as those of customers. Furthermore, work arrangements that were flexible and collegial supported mutual adjustments beyond formal work systems. The repetition of similar clustering pattern[s] contributed to the mapping of practices described in the literature as 'high performance work systems'.
>
> (Verreynne *et al.*, 2013: 420)

This insight builds on the value of talking to employees as well as owner-managers since, as Verreynne *et al.* (2013: 423) suggest, employees, in contrast to the owner-managers, are immersed in these informal practices that control their working behaviours and govern their approaches to work, appreciating their impacts on performance, productivity and job satisfaction. Verreynne and colleagues focus on informality in terms of how it facilitates flexibility, suggesting some of the ways in which mutual adjustment and adaptation to external forces and particular challenges can be productive for a business.

The nature of studies that fail to engage with informal practices can also misrepresent relatively formal practices that do not require formal policies, plans or prescriptions. Scott *et al.* (1989: 34) coined the term *informal routinisation* to describe a common approach to people management in SMEs. This reflects how these organisations establish practices through experience and over time rather than deriving them from formal policies, and it suggests how some studies of HPWS risk confusing formal and operative organisational structures (Ford and Schellenberg, 1982). If we are to understand practices in SMEs, we have to attend to the ways in which the everyday practices that create these operative organisational structures can develop over time to be in frequent and regular use without formal policies setting out what is to be done and how (Wright and Boswell, 2002).

Even if, as Sheehan (2014) suggests, SMEs are becoming more formal, the broad range of descriptions of practices in use that we have discussed throughout this book suggests that we have to get to grips with informal ways of working if we are to understand how SMEs operate. Further, if we want to take a performative approach and focus on those practices that are effective, we suggest that it is still valuable to consider both formal and informal practices in their immediate contexts and in relation to the challenges they seek to overcome.

*The persistence of a deficit model?*

The starting point for the types of study of HRM and performance discussed in this chapter, such as those on HPWS, can be an idealised model of management rather than the everyday employment relationships and practices of SMEs. For example, while Sheehan valuably piloted her study to choose which practices to focus on (dropping job security and harmonisation as less relevant to SMEs), the practices examined in this pilot were those derived from studies of large firms. As Sheehan explains:

> in order to examine whether the well-evidenced positive relationship between human resources and performance is found in the SME context, focus is given to formal human resource practices, and thereby the potentially significant role of informal practices could not be captured.
>
> (Sheehan, 2014: 553)

That is, her starting point is to seek to replicate findings from large firms in SMEs. Such a perspective is also found in Greer *et al.*'s (2015) recent work focusing on recruitment practices and small-firm performance. Greer *et al.*, ignoring the lessons from Bacon and colleagues (1996) about over-claiming when it comes to reporting certain management practices, suggest that small firms should adopt recruitment approaches associated with large businesses. Although they recognise that '[s]mall firms are different from larger firms in ways that have not been fully understood by HR researchers, and the practices that may work well in them may be ineffective in large firms' (Greer et al., 2015: 18), they do not engage with suggestions that this limitation might also run in the opposite direction (Heneman and Berkley, 1999).

We have argued throughout the book that we should, instead, consider in what ways SMEs may be distinct from large firms and examine these differences on their own terms. We do not argue that there are no commonalities, nor that mainstream HRM practices will not be of value to some SMEs. Rather, we emphasise that it is necessary to understand SMEs' employment relationships and practices in use and evaluate them in context, avoiding the trap of the deficit model (see Chapters 4 and 5) which encourages comparison with implicitly idealised large-firm practices. Similarly, where SMEs do make effective use of large-firm practices there is no reason to assume that this represents an ideal that all SMEs should aspire to emulate. As Gilman and Edwards have argued:

> Claims to identify a specific 'thing' such as an HPWS are certainly unhelpful, but some of the underlying ideas around the organization of people are useful. We thus follow some critics of the HPWS view, who argue for a contextualized understanding of 'good management' (Godard, 2004; Paauwe, 2004), and also students of small firms who aim to understand concrete practice in its own terms, rather than arguing that small firms 'fail' to follow a correct model (Storey and Westhead, 1997; Taylor, 2006).
> 
> (Gilman and Edwards, 2008: 532)

Unfortunately, many studies of HPWS and similar approaches to HRM tend not to differentiate adequately contextual factors or even firm size. Nevertheless, we can often identify the types of firm that may be most appropriate to the studies. For example, in Sheehan's (2014) study, she focused on firms with 10–249 employees, in line with common definitions of SMEs, though excluding the self-employed (where any management or 'employment' is likely to be informal and unaccounted for) and micro firms (together constituting the vast majority of businesses in the UK). Further, she identified that '[t]he only statistically significant response bias found was for firms that employed fewer than 25 people: these were statistically significantly less likely to participate in either survey at the 0.05 percent level' (ibid.: 553). That is, the firms employing fewer than 25 staff (the next biggest group after those initially excluded) were potentially not representative of the broader population of similarly sized businesses.

Sheehan then excluded firms less than 18 months old, on the reasonable assumption that new firms would be too 'idiosyncratic' (Sheehan, 2014: 552).

By excluding these younger firms at her first measuring point (2007), this meant that the firms that also participated in the second survey (2011) had, at this point, been operating for a minimum of five years. This is potentially problematic given the high failure rates among firms in their first five years (see analysis by Coad et al., 2013). Taken together, these sampling issues, which may appear esoteric and statistical, actually suggest a significant misrepresentation of the general population of SMEs.

These problems do not necessarily discount the rigour of Sheehan's study, or the value of her findings, but they do suggest limitations in their applicability to all but a small, specific subset of firms. As we might perhaps expect, those firms that have been relatively successful, in existence for a number of years and with a relatively high number of employees may be more likely to engage effectively with HRM approaches derived from large businesses. This may help to explain why the SMEs Sheehan studied seemed more formal than generally assumed. It highlights that we need to be particularly careful when considering small and medium-sized businesses together (Hoque and Bacon, 2008) and, importantly, it does not provide compelling evidence that the majority of smaller businesses should mimic those firms for which Sheehan identified high performance. Without a clear understanding of contextual factors and the particular challenges faced, it is difficult to know at what point or in what ways the policies or practices Sheehan studied become valuable.

## Employment relationships in SMEs

It is certainly reasonable to assume that for some SMEs, especially those that are medium sized, established and with significant resources, HPWS could be appropriate and supply a competitive advantage – that is, for those SMEs that share characteristics with the large firms for which such systems were designed. However, even here, we should be cautious about over-generalising. For example, Purcell (1999: 36), writing about this area of HRM research more generally, argues:

> The claim that the bundle of best practice HRM is universally applicable leads us into a utopian cul-de-sac and ignores the powerful and highly significant changes in work, employment and society visible inside organisations and in the wider community. The search for bundles of high commitment work practices is important, but so too is the search for understanding of the circumstances of where and when it is applied, why some organisations do and others do not adopt HCM [high commitment management], and how some firms seem to have more appropriate HR systems for their current and future needs than others.

This appears particularly heightened in the case of SMEs. For those firms that do not share key characteristics with large firms, we suggest, in line with critiques of the deficit model perspective, that working 'downwards' from a sense of a large firm ideal is not the best way to understand the practices in use in smaller businesses or how to optimise the effectiveness of these practices. Even for a high-growth-oriented firm that aspires to the size and form or organisation for which HPWS would perhaps be suitable, there is no evidence to suggest that implementing these systems at an early stage of the firm's development (and especially at start-up) would make these aspirations any more achievable.

As opposed to the homogenising and prescriptive approach of using HPWS to shape employment relationships and practices in SMEs, we advocate starting with the employment relationships and practices as a basis for understanding. Adopting this perspective has value, especially in SMEs, because it enables us to appreciate the relationships constituting working lives, rather than just focusing on policies that are intended to organise or govern it. Through this perspective, as highlighted in Chapter 1, we can make sense of employment relationships and practices in SMEs as 'processes through which employers and employees – who are tied together in relations of mutual dependence underlain by exploitation – negotiate the performance of work tasks, together with the laws, rules, agreements and customs that shape these processes' (Edwards, 1995: 47). In the next, final chapter, we draw out in greater detail the implications of this view for how employment relationships and practices in SMEs are understood.

## Conclusion

This chapter has critically discussed a currently popular area of research into the management of human resources in SMEs: high performance work systems (HPWS). We have described how these studies have examined bundles or packages of management practices and their effect on performance. These studies have had mixed results, with some suggesting implications for owner-managers seeking a competitive advantage (Sheehan, 2014), while others have suggested the possibility that costs of such systems may outweigh the benefits (Way, 2002; Sels et al., 2006b). Overall, it has been claimed that 'the relationship between HRM and firm performance remains fuzzy and results depend on the population sampled and the measures used' (Sels et al., 2006a: 319).

We have explored these mixed findings through a critique of the HPWS and SME literature, drawing on some of the key insights developed through our examination of SME practices throughout the book. This critique has suggested particular problems and limitations with this research around assessing the presence and impacts of HRM, employee experiences and informality, and a persistent failure to leave behind the deficit model. In the final chapter we draw out these and other key themes from the book that allow us to understand what tends to be distinctive about SMEs and to gain some insights into their employment relationships and practices.

# 10 Conclusion
## The management of human resources in SMEs

An important consideration in the study of SMEs, which has formed a central concern for this book, is their heterogeneity. While we can label firms with a specific number of employees or level of financial turnover 'small' or 'medium-sized' (or, for that matter, 'large') for convenience, the benefits are quickly outweighed by the problems of size determinism, where firms are grouped on the basis of size and are then assumed to be alike in other respects (Torrès and Julien, 2005). Size determinism presents significant problems if we want to conduct any meaningful analysis of how businesses operate. As highlighted in Chapter 1, and, we hope, has become clear through the following chapters, firms that share the characteristic of similar size cannot be simply assumed to share similarities in terms of the employment relationships and practices we might find within them or the wider contexts in which they operate (Barrett and Rainnie, 2002; Ram and Edwards, 2003).

We are, then, faced with something of a problem. On the one hand, we maintain that there are some similarities between firms employing similar numbers of people – after all, we are making the distinction on employee numbers and have suggested that this is relevant to the employment relationships and practices we have explored throughout the book. On the other hand, we need to avoid the kind of size determinism against which authors such as Rainnie have warned. Such issues have been explored, as identified in Chapter 1, through the debate played out between Torrès and Julien (2005) and Curran (2006). Both positions are valid and represent important concerns, so how can they be balanced to enable us to move beyond the lack of analytical focus produced by heterogeneity without collapsing firms of similar sizes into a single homogenous category?

This concluding chapter will attempt to answer this question by setting out some themes that have emerged through our discussion of various HR practices throughout the book and which help to characterise what we perceive as interesting and potentially different about SMEs. What these themes allow us to achieve is to consider how a particular small or medium-sized enterprise may differ from the models of organisations driving mainstream understandings of human resource management practices.

For any given firm, one characteristic may be heightened in its relevance while another becomes less important. For some firms, the idealised model of human resource management that is derived from mainstream textbooks and larger businesses may be wholly relevant and useful, while for other firms this idealised model will be of no value at all. What matters is the appreciation of the potential for difference and heterogeneity, and our proposed themes seek to help to make sense of these differences and how employment relationships and practices may develop in SMEs.

In Chapter 1 we outlined three characteristics common to many SMEs: a high degree of informality; close social and spatial proximity; and resource poverty. Each of these characteristics has implications for the ways in which employment relationships and practices are conducted on a day-to-day basis. It is worth briefly restating what we mean by these characteristics:

1   A high degree of informality: an absence or limited use of written policies and practices, an ad hoc way of organising and distributing tasks rather than clearly defined job roles.
2   Close social and spatial proximity: where owner-managers and employees work alongside each other there is scope for overlap between personal and working relationships and a greater degree of familiarity in the workplace.
3   Resource poverty: smaller firms tend to be concentrated in industries subject to price cutting, the relative burden of owner-managers' salaries on revenues tends to be greater, they are more vulnerable to internal errors and external shocks, and find it more difficult to exert influence on their external environment.

In this final chapter we want to build on these characteristics to suggest the themes that have emerged through the book's discussion of SME practices and which help us to characterise these businesses in a more detailed, analytical way. The themes we will discuss in this chapter are: the politicisation of SMEs; the need to analyse SME practices on their own terms; the interaction of external and internal influences; the interactions between policy and practice; the tensions involved in mutual adjustment; and, finally, the dynamic, direct and indirect effects of external influences. Each section below discusses a theme and highlights a *key insight* derived from our analysis for you to reflect on further. We will conclude by drawing on these themes to suggest potential ways forward in considering SMEs in terms of research, policy and practice.

## Theme one: the politicisation of SMEs

One way in which SMEs differ from larger firms, and which can have important consequences, is in terms of the ways in which they are represented and discussed politically. We discussed this in Chapter 3, where we drew on Dannreuther and Perren's (2013a, 2013b) work that has described the ways in which SMEs have been defined and utilised in politics. For example, when small firms emerged into political debates more prominently in the 1960s, it was in becoming part of a larger debate around closing tax loop holes with small firms identified as particularly vulnerable to tax (Bolton, 1971). In this way, the importance of small firms was used to support a particular political aim (simplification or reduction of the tax system). What defines a small firm in the context of particular political agendas had (and continues to have) important implications for SME research and practice.

In contemporary international debates, SMEs are presented as the downtrodden heroes of the modern economy, determined to grow but assailed from all sides by challenges to sap their strength, confuse their minds and slow their progress. Rainnie (1985) frames this as small firms being cast as simultaneously both the 'small furry animals' of the economy, needing support and assistance, and the 'shock troops' that will return the economy to prosperity. Political discourse surrounding SMEs suggests that there are correct ways to be an entrepreneur in the pursuit of growth and correct sources from which to seek support and assistance (such as accountants, bankers) who reinforce these assumptions and instil forms of dependency (Gibb, 2000). Within such a narrow sense of what an SME is, expectations become established for ambitions and performance goals, and therefore particular assumptions about what constitutes success. This can distort research and subsequent understandings of these businesses in the ways we discussed in Chapters 8 and 9.

These ways of thinking about SMEs have been deployed by a range of different political agendas – for example, in the UK, from the individualism of Thatcher to the proposed inclusion and social justice of New Labour. Politically, SMEs therefore have become viewed as central to Britain's knowledge-based, liberal market economy and part of an increasingly broad range of political debates, with similar impacts and implications internationally. These implications can be seen, for example, in terms of government approaches to regulation (see, e.g., Chapter 7), the development of bodies such as Investors in People and other areas unrelated to the focus of this book, such as access to finance. This has important implications for SMEs in terms of the external influences operating on the business, especially as many SMEs do not have the resources or influence to challenge or shape these debates. It also effects the ways in which ownermanagers and their employees may think about the business – for example, that it is in some way deficient if not pursuing growth.

> *Key insight*: Dominant understandings of SMEs are heavily influenced by politics, shaping the expectations and focus of owner-managers, employees and academic researchers.

## Theme two: the need to analyse SME practices on their own terms

In Chapter 4, we highlighted what Behrends (2007) has termed the 'deficit' and 'equivalence' models of understanding employment practices in SMEs.

Under a deficit perspective 'there is an implicit assumption that formal policies must prevail' (Harney and Dundon, 2007: 111), and comparisons are made with the practices of large firms' HR departments. A large firm ideal is used, implicitly or explicitly, as the benchmark against which practices in SMEs are evaluated. This creates a problem because rather than focusing on questions of whether practices are achieving their objectives within a given context, the question is subtly reframed to become one of how far SME practices resemble an idealised image derived from a (no doubt sanitised, formally rational and generic) representation of what should happen in larger organisations.

This may lead an SME to adopt large-firm policies, or the idea of formalised human resource management policies and practices more generally, as that is the 'right' thing to do (i.e. attempting to overcome the deficit). If this is not the appropriate response for a particular firm facing particular challenges, such an approach could damage the business and its operations – for example, in the case of reward systems and other policies that are imported from large organisations but inappropriate for effective performance management within SMEs. In this example, in organisations with close spatial and social proximity, it may be the case that performance management occurs on a frequent basis through regular interactions and a close monitoring of work. Where this is the case, such practices can undermine more formal appraisal systems. The point we want to make here is that while there may be limitations to such informal performance management (for example in maintaining equity), they can be effective and may be the most appropriate approach for some firms. We suggest studying these practices in use in terms of their effectiveness in context rather than in contrast with the practices proposed for much larger, and potentially very different businesses.

A further concern with the deficit perspective is that it can narrow our focus when we consider employment relationships and practices in SMEs. If we are continually comparing the practices we find against a supposed ideal of 'best practice', the temptation is to identify only those practices that can fit into that frame of reference *rather than* seeking out practices in use, understanding what they are intended to achieve, how and why and with what results. We can see this, for example, in some of the survey studies discussed in Chapter 9, where owner-managers were asked about the presence of specific practices the researchers had derived from large-firm studies. Using an inappropriate benchmark of practice succeeds only in telling us that a given firm is not like a large firm (bad) or is behaving like a large firm (good). It does not help us to understand a great deal about employment relationships and practices in SMEs, the issues encountered or how they are addressed.

> *Key insight*: We need to be wary of applying insights from large firms to smaller firms and judging SMEs against these idealised representations. Instead, it is vital to understand what works for SMEs, and to bear in mind their heterogeneity.

## Theme three: the interaction of external and internal influences

'SME' can be an unhelpful label in that it masks such a huge array of difference. In Chapter 3 we sought to orient readers by putting organisations into context. We cannot start getting to grips with understanding employment relationships and practices in firms unless we have some appreciation of how they sit in relation to the various influences in firms' external and internal environments. We outlined the work of Gilman and Edwards (2008) and their framework in Chapter 3 in order to guide reflection on this idea.

Where this framework is particularly helpful is in attending to the heterogeneity of SMEs by identifying seven key dimensions: product market; labour market; resources; strategic choice; rules and routines; management style; and networks. Where some dimensions will be particularly salient for some enterprises, other dimensions will be key to understanding a different firm or operating context. By identifying that a wide range of influences help to shape employment issues in SMEs, we can avoid over-attributing employment relationships to a single class of influence or actors. In this regard, Al Rainnie's (1989) work has been criticised for over-emphasising the influence that is exerted by large firms. Building on Rainnie's important insights by considering them as part of a broader context, we highlighted the perspectives outlined by Monder Ram, Paul Edwards and colleagues which focus on how a range of influences come into play to shape employment relationships and practices in SMEs. We have suggested, and explored through several set tasks, how these influences can be valuably analysed using the Gilman and Edwards (2008) framework.

Recognising whether influences arise externally or internally to the firm is useful. However, given that SMEs, and especially small firms, may not have the resources to shape their external environment in the same way as large businesses potentially can, it is important to focus on the interaction of the different influences to facilitate greater analytical depth. The extent to which considerations such as labour markets exert influence on firms and give rise to responses that shape their employment relationships and practices helps us to understand what might underlie the practices in use. An explicit feature of Harney and Dundon's (2006) contribution on this topic is a feedback loop from the HRM outcomes back into the point of interaction between external and internal influences. The inclusion of this loop helpfully illustrates that employment relationships and practices in SMEs can be understood as an ongoing, everyday process of adjustment.

By seeking to understand the employment relationships and practices of SMEs in terms of the interactions between different external and internal influences, we enter an area of significant complexity. To build a detailed appreciation of how these businesses are organised we need to be attentive to their contexts, the issues they encounter, and the responses arising that influence the shape of their employment relationships and practices. Our starting point is that we need to take SMEs as we find them and build our understanding from the perspective of the firms we study. The literature featured in this book, such as Marchington et al. (2003), demonstrates how this approach helps to develop our understanding.

> *Key insight*: A range of external and internal factors interact to influence employment relationships and practices in SMEs, some of which may be particularly salient in some firms but less so in others.

## Theme four: the interactions between policy and practice

In our chapter on training and development (Chapter 5), we raised the issue of formal and informal practices and used this to highlight an important distinction in the study of SMEs, between policy and practice. We suggest that confusing policy and practice rests on an assumption that the former is reflected straightforwardly in the latter. Using the example of Investors in People accreditation, we argued that formal policies can serve purposes beyond strictly operational concerns. In the cases we have studied, as in Ram (2000), the formal account of training practices in firms is not necessarily a record of practices in use and is not intended to be. To treat the existence of formal policy as indicative of practices in use is to misunderstand how they are distinct and how they may serve different purposes within an organisation.

The distinction between policy and practice is important because our understanding of this distinction has implications for how we get to grips with employment relationships and practices in SMEs. Formal policies are easier to identify than practices in use. While the former can be pulled from the shelf, the latter must be recognised, interpreted and understood over time. If we assume that formal policies represent practices in use then we might be satisfied once we have gathered the available policies or asked an owner-manager about their utilisation of formal HRM processes. An implication of this is that where policies cannot be found or do not exist, it might be assumed that nothing is occurring, *rather than* shifting our mindset to consider the practices in use – clearly an untenable position.

This partly reflects a need to understand the practices in a firm but also to take these into account when choosing or implementing policies. It is not only about a deficit model but about understanding how practices will be altered, or even push back against the policy itself. The informal and formal aspects of organisations co-exist, as discussed in Chapter 8, and this means they will interact and influence, advance or undermine each other. For example, formal selection criteria can be informally amended or suspended due to trust in a personal recommendation or for the hiring of a friend or family member. Similarly, informal practices cannot be ignored or overridden when choosing, implementing or assessing formal policies. So, we should not assume that policies provide the full picture of organisational practices, and instead we should seek to understand the ways in which policies and practices interact to produce organisational outcomes.

*Key insight*: Policies and practices (whether formal or informal) interact and can have complex outcomes that escape simple description or superficial understanding.

## Theme five: the tensions involved in mutual adjustment

In Chapter 6 we considered the idea of owner-manager prerogative and, in particular, the limits to viewing firms as necessarily dominated by owner-managers. A traditional view of the internal working of small firms is that they reflect the owner-manager's wishes and are, in effect, an extension of their personality (Goss, 1991; Beaver, 2003). Under this view, the owner-manager of the firm sets the direction for the business to follow and the rules that govern how to get there. The autocratic owner-manager (see Goss, 1991) undoubtedly exists and reinforces the possibility of worker exploitation in SMEs but, as we highlighted in Chapter 3, over-attribution of effects to any single cause (external or internal to the firm) can limit our understanding of practices that are typically produced through complex interactions of multiple influences.

Within the firm there are degrees of competing (and complementary) interests, perhaps most fundamentally, but not exclusively, between what owners might want and what employees might hope for. Resolving these competing interests in the small firm context has been attributed to processes of mutual adjustment (Ram, 1999) and ongoing, everyday negotiation (Wapshott and Mallett, 2013). This process, embedded in the tension between autonomy and control, is characterised by an element of give and take, as parties seek to obtain an acceptable level of satisfaction given their circumstances. Importantly, these forms of negotiation may not be formal, or even explicitly acknowledged, and may interact with external influences such as the labour market or clients' need for stability. For example, an employee who is valued by an external client and difficult to replace in the labour market may hold a relatively high degree of perceived value such that the firm's owner-manager may anticipate their seeking to exert the influence this grants them, therefore pre-emptively providing them with some form of reward to avoid this.

The processes of mutual adjustment facilitated by close social and spatial proximity can create variety in the kinds of employment relationships and practices found within organisations or even particular parts of organisations. Adjustments might be made mindful of considerations such as maintaining a harmonious workplace, avoiding disruptive cycles of staff turnover and recruitment, or trying to retain staff members who generate income for the business. This variation represents an important element in the heterogeneity of SMEs, highlighting the need to understand the internal dynamics of these firms and not simply see their employment relationships or practices as determined by powerful external forces.

*Key insight*: Employment relationships and working practices in SMEs are the outcome of ongoing, everyday negotiations, often in a context of close spatial and social proximity.

## Theme six: the dynamic, direct and indirect effects of external influences

Our emphasis on internal negotiation is not to downplay external influences but, rather, to highlight that we cannot understand how employment relationships and practices develop without understanding what is happening inside the firm. So, for external influences, ongoing, everyday negotiation moderates the ways in which external factors influence the organisation through dynamic, direct and indirect effects.

We have discussed employment regulation at several points throughout the book, for example in Chapter 7 in relation to staff exit and employee turnover. The matter of employment regulation and SMEs is interesting empirically because, as Carter *et al.* (2009: 276) argue, 'regulation has attracted more attention than is justified by its significance', and consequently draws resources and attention away from debating 'issues that genuinely impinge on the vitality of the small business sector'. Nonetheless, the debate around understanding the impacts and effects of regulation on SMEs is important in and of itself. It also helps us to think about how SMEs accommodate external pressures more generally.

Regulation with the weight of legal enforcement stands as a potentially important form of external influence yet, as we have discussed in a variety of contexts, this influence is not straightforward. For example, in relation to a national minimum wage, we discussed in Chapter 6 how variable the effects of this regulation were. Where some firms implemented changes to their employees' pay, even if already paying above the minimum rate, others made adjustments to recorded working hours or to breaks, while others engaged in work intensification to recover costs (Gilman *et al.*, 2002). This variation reflects the heterogeneity of SMEs but also the unpredictability of external influences due to their dynamic, direct and indirect effects (Kitching *et al.*, 2013; Kitching *et al.*, 2015). For example, where the introduction of a minimum wage rate increases employment costs, the different ways owner-managers may try to recover these costs, such as cutting break times, represent an indirect result of the regulation. There may be other types of indirect influence such as regulatory compliance requiring an increasingly formal approach to the employment relationship more generally, as suggested by Sheehan (2014) and discussed in Chapter 9.

> *Key insight*: Even powerful external influences will not have universal effects on SMEs and must, instead, be understood as dynamic, direct and indirect, moderated by the ongoing, everyday negotiation of the employment relationships within the firm.

## The future of HRM in SMEs

Small and medium-sized firms are not homogeneous but have tendencies that mean they differ (by degree if not in kind) from many larger businesses (Ram *et al.*, 2001). Importantly, these differences do not mean that SMEs are deficient but, rather, that we cannot simply import our understanding of large firms to make sense of them. The themes we have highlighted above do not represent an exhaustive list, but rather are those themes that emerged as particularly relevant to the analysis of practices throughout this book. Most importantly, this is rooted in the argument that we need to understand SME employment relationships and practices on their own terms. In this section we draw on the key insights outlined above to suggest some possible implications for how we might think about the future of managing human resources in SMEs in terms of research, policy and practice.

## Research

The past 40 years or so have witnessed a rapid rise in the attention paid to SMEs, and particularly to the employment relationships and practices we associate with such firms. It can no longer really be said that there is a shortage of research on this topic. However, there is a great deal still to be learnt and there are real opportunities to engage with a field that features interesting empirical and conceptual work.

In order to develop a more detailed understanding of practices in use, we would like to see more empirically rich ethnographic studies that seek to understand and explain the employment relationships and practices found in SMEs in different contexts (for classic examples, see Ram, 1994; Holliday, 1995). Further in-depth studies of businesses featuring different owner-managers and employees – for example, in terms of their age, gender or ethnic backgrounds, different national contexts, industry sectors and so on – could bring not only richness to the field but help us understand the boundaries of current explanations, highlighting where new thinking is required.

Building on the need for more ethnographic study of SMEs, we also believe there is scope for more longitudinal work to be conducted. Many small and new businesses, in particular, face turbulent and hostile environments that can overwhelm them, resulting in business closure. Yet, there is often a sense of relative stability in studies of employment relationships and practices which fails to reflect the challenges, change and crises we might expect. While, for example, Sheehan's (2014) study (discussed in Chapter 9) valuably provided a longitudinal aspect by focusing only on those relatively rare firms that survived their first five years of operating, her findings obscure the majority of firms that do not succeed, or survive in different ways such as through entering the informal economy. Longitudinal studies of HRM in SMEs could capture how businesses encounter the challenges of survival and contribute to understanding in this part of the field.

We hope that further detailed and longitudinal work can take businesses and practices as they find them. By this we mean moving away from an occasional, but persistent, sense in which SMEs are viewed as deficient relative to larger businesses and the policies associated with them. Moreover, research should resist pressures to assume that all enterprises are pursuing growth, or would if they could. Unless research can speak to those who operate, manage and work in SMEs and engage with their everyday practices rather than a normative discourse, researchers may find themselves increasingly commentating from the sidelines of enterprise rather than making worthwhile contributions to understanding how enterprises operate and the experiences of those working within them.

## Government policy

SMEs are politically popular: just try finding a politician who will say anything against these enterprises! Robert J. Bennett's (2014) book (in this Routledge series) offers a fascinating account of how politics in the USA plays a role in the dealings of that country's Small Business Administration, indicating the problems of political interventions for SMEs. Bennett's book highlights the difficulties of designing and delivering effective SME policy but emphasises the need to empower this constituency politically and make the delivery of policy and government support more diffuse, reaching beyond the targets of larger SMEs and including micro firms. From our narrower perspective on employment relationships and practices, we have discussed how rhetoric around SMEs, for example in relation to employment regulation, often exacerbates these problems through an apparent ignorance of research findings commenting on its impacts. As Carter et al. (2009) suggest, focusing attention and energy on something like the negative effects of regulation, which seem to affect relatively few SMEs, might just be distracting from developing interventions to tackle real problems.

During their long exclusion from political debate and academic research, SMEs were left without definition and the protections of regulation, allowing poor pay and working conditions. However, the later exploitation of SMEs in political discourse has allowed politicians to legitimise their activities and ambitions, for example through the ways in which '[r]isk was rhetorically dissipated from the centralised state to the individual through the device of small firm policy' (Dannreuther and Perren, 2013a: 167). Instead of this tactical deployment of SMEs to justify ideologically driven policy, we hope to see a reduction in rhetoric driven by political beliefs and greater attention paid to the detail and nuance of empirical research in this area. Of course, this also needs researchers to move beyond the politically hot topics such as business growth. Granted, such a shift might complicate the political message but it would at least engage with the everyday practices and experiences of SMEs.

## Practice

As academics, the 'implications for practice' section should be approached with some trepidation, if not humility. Research forays and other interests aside, academics typically work in very large organisations. From our studies of SMEs, however, we can offer some suggestions or reflections for those who earn a living through running or working in an SME.

Our starting point is to underline that different is not necessarily deficient. Operating along relatively informal lines, within the law, may suit a business and its employees. There might be little gained by yielding to perceived pressures to adopt formal management systems around, for example, performance-related pay. Implementing standard HRM practices simply to portray some impression of 'proper' practices and legitimacy without tailoring them to suit the enterprise can be detrimental. The acid test remains whether a particular practice, whether or not underpinned by policy, makes sense for a given enterprise. Doing things differently from typical prescriptions does not necessarily mean that a business or an approach is lacking. Throughout the book we have outlined a broad range of studies and cases that suggest potentially effective practices in response to different challenges and contexts but, as we hope has become clear, there is no simple prescription for what constitutes best practices for SMEs. Those working within SMEs need to engage with their particular challenges and contexts to work out what practices work best for them.

## Managing human resources in small and medium-sized enterprises

The common theme to the areas discussed above, and throughout the book, is to question underlying assumptions, principally in relation to the assumption that large-firm HR practices are an ideal to be aspired to and can be transplanted into SMEs. Instead, we suggest that researchers, policymakers and those working in SMEs should apply a standard of what works ahead of what is perceived as somehow legitimate. Doubtless, this approach introduces greater complexity than deploying very broad 'one-size-fits-all' interpretations of employment relationships and practices in small and medium-sized enterprises, but the benefits of a deeper understanding make this worthwhile − for example, by creating opportunities for more relevant interventions in firms.

The primary aim of this book has been to offer an accessible but detailed discussion of employment relationships and practices in SMEs. We have drawn on a range of international literature to draw out and discuss a range of key points. However, as we conclude the book, we re-emphasise that it has been intended as a starting point for your own exploration and study of SMEs' employment relationships and practices. We hope that this book has prompted you to think differently and more deeply about SMEs and has given you some encouragement to pursue the further development of your own ideas.

# Bibliography

Abbott, B. (1993) 'Training strategies in small service sector firms: employer and employee perspectives', *Human Resource Management Journal*, 4(2), pp. 70–87.
Abor, J. and Quartey, P. (2010) 'Issues in SME development in Ghana and South Africa', *International Research Journal of Finance and Economics*, 39(6), pp. 218–228.
Adler, P.S. (1995) 'Interdepartmental interdependence and coordination: the case of the design/manufacturing interface', *Organization Science*, 6(2), pp. 147–167.
Ahmed, K. and Chowdhury, T.A. (2009) 'Performance evaluation of SMEs of Bangladesh', *International Journal of Business and Management*, 4(7), pp. 126–133.
Allen, M.R., Ericksen, J. and Collins, C.J. (2013) 'Human resource management, employee exchange relationships, and performance in small businesses', *Human Resource Management*, 52(2), pp. 153–174.
Anyadike-Danes, M., Bonner, K. and Hart, M. (2011) Job creation and destruction in the UK: 1998–2010, Economics & Strategy Group Aston Business School, August 2011. www.gov.uk/government/uploads/system/uploads/attachment_data/file/32244/11-1326-job-creation-and-destruction-uk-1998-2010.pdf (accessed 15 March 2015).
Aragón-Sánchez, A., Barba-Aragón, I. and Sanz-Valle, R. (2003) 'Effects of training on business results', *The International Journal of Human Resource Management*, 14(6), pp. 956–980.
Arrowsmith, J., Gilman, M.W., Edwards, P. and Ram, M. (2003) 'The impact of the National Minimum Wage in small firms', *British Journal of Industrial Relations*, 41(3), pp. 435–456.
Arrowsmith, J. and Sisson, K. (1999) 'Pay and working time: towards organization-based systems?', *British Journal of Industrial Relations*, 37(1), pp. 51–75.
Atkinson, C. (2008) 'An exploration of small firm psychological contracts', *Work, Employment & Society*, 22(3), pp. 447–465.
Atkinson, C. and Curtis, S. (2004), 'The impact of employment regulation on the employment relationship in SMEs', *Journal of Small Business and Enterprise Development*, 11(4), pp. 486–494.
Atkinson, C., Mallett, O. and Wapshott, R. (2014) '"You try to be a fair employer": regulation and employment relationships in medium-sized firms', *International Small Business Journal* online 17 July. http://isb.sagepub.com/content/early/2014/07/17/0266242614541992.full.pdf+html (accessed 15 March 2015).
Bacon, N., Ackers, P., Storey, J. and Coates, D. (1996) 'It's a small world: managing human resources in small businesses', *The International Journal of Human Resource Management*, 7(1), pp. 83–100.

Baines, S. and Wheelock, J. (1998) 'Reinventing traditional solutions: job creation, gender and the micro-business household', *Work, Employment & Society*, 12(4), pp. 579–601.

Barney, J. (1991) 'Firm resources and sustained competitive advantage', *Journal of Management*, 17(1), pp. 99–120.

Baron, R.A. (2003) 'Human resource management and entrepreneurship: some reciprocal benefits of closer links', *Human Resource Management Review*, 13, pp. 253–256.

Barrett, R. (2008) 'Small business learning through mentoring: evaluating a project', *Education + Training*, 48(8/9), pp. 614–626.

Barrett, R. and Rainnie, A. (2002) 'What's so special about small firms? Developing an integrated approach to analysing small firm industrial relations', *Work, Employment and Society*, 16(3), pp. 415–431.

Baum, J.A.C. (1996) 'Organizational ecology.' In Clegg, S., Hardy, C. and Nord, W.R. (eds) *Handbook of organization studies*. London: SAGE Publications, pp. 77–114.

Beaumont, P.B., Hunter, L.C. and Sinclair, D. (1996) 'Customer-supplier relations and the diffusion of employee relations changes', *Employee Relations*, 18(1), pp. 9–19.

Beaver, G. (2003) 'Editorial: management and the small firm', *Strategic Change*, 12(2), pp. 63–68.

Beaver, G. and Prince, C. (2004) 'Management, strategy and policy in the UK small business sector: a critical review', *Journal of Small Business and Enterprise Development*, 11(1), pp. 34–49.

Beckman, C.M. and Burton, M.D. (2008) 'Founding the future: path dependence in the evolution of top management teams from founding to IPO', *Organization Science*, 19(1), pp. 3–24.

Behrends, T. (2007) 'Recruitment practices in small and medium size enterprises. An empirical study among knowledge-intensive professional service firms', *Management Revue*, 18(1), pp. 55–74.

Bendix, R. (1956) *Work and authority in industry: ideologies of management in the course of industrialization*. London: Chapman & Hall Ltd.

Bennett, R.J. (2014) *Entrepreneurship, small business and public policy: evolution and revolution*. Abingdon: Routledge.

Beynon, M.J., Jones, P., Pickernell, D. and Packham, D. (2015) 'Investigating the impact of training influence on employee retention in small and medium enterprises: a regression-type classification and ranking believe simplex analysis on sparse data', *Expert Systems*, 32(1), pp. 141–154.

Birley, S. and Westhead, P. (1990) 'Growth and performance contrasts between "types" of small firms', *Strategic Management Journal*, 11(7), pp. 535–557.

BIS (2013) *Workplace Employment Relations Study (WERS) information page*. www.gov.uk/government/collections/workplace-employment-relations-study-wers (accessed 2 January 2015).

BIS (2014) *Business population estimates for the UK and regions 2014*. Department for Business, Innovation and Skills, 26 November. www.gov.uk/government/uploads/system/uploads/attachment_data/file/377934/bpe_2014_statistical_release.pdf (accessed 15 March 2015).

Bischoff, C. and Wood, G. (2013) 'Selective informality: the self-limiting growth choices of small businesses in South Africa', *International Labour Review*, 152(3–4), pp. 493–505.

Blackburn, R., Edwards, P., Storey, D., Saridakis, G. and Sen-Gupta, S. (2007) 'The analysis of SMEs and some methodological challenges.' In Whitfield, K. and Huxley, K.

(eds) *Innovations in the 2004 workplace employment relations survey.* Cardiff: Cardiff University, pp.119–145.

Bolton, J.E. (1971) *Small firms: report of the committee of inquiry on small firms.* London: HMSO. Cmnd. 4811.

Bratton, J. and Gold, J. (1999) *Human resource management: theory and practice.* Basingstoke: Palgrave Macmillan.

Breslin, D. (2010) 'Broadening the management team: an evolutionary approach', *International Journal of Entrepreneurial Behaviour & Research*, 16(2), pp. 130–148.

Bryan, J. (2006) 'Training and performance in small firms', *International Small Business Journal*, 24(6), pp. 635–660.

Burns, P. and Harrison, J. (1996) 'Growth.' In Burns, P. and Dewhurst, J. (eds) *Small business and entrepreneurship* (2nd edn). Basingstoke: Palgrave Macmillan, pp. 40–72.

Cameron, D. (2014) *Speech to Federation of Small Businesses*, 27 January. www.gov.uk/government/news/supporting-business-david-cameron-announces-new-plans (accessed 14 March 2015).

Cardon, M.S. and Stevens, C.E. (2004) 'Managing human resources in small organizations: what do we know?', *Human Resource Management Review*, 14(3), pp. 295–323.

Carroll, M., Marchington, M., Earnshaw, J. and Taylor, S. (1999) 'Recruitment in small firms: processes, methods, and problems', *Employee Relations*, 21(3), pp. 236–250.

Carter, S., Mason, C. and Tagg, S. (2009) 'Perceptions and experience of employment regulation in UK small firms', *Environment and Planning C: Government and Policy*, 27(2), pp. 263–278.

Cassell, C., Nadin, S., Gray, M. and Clegg, C. (2002) 'Exploring human resource management practices in small and medium sized enterprises', *Personnel Review*, 31(6), pp. 671–692.

Charan, R., Hofer, C.W. and Mahon, J.F. (1980) 'From entrepreneurial to professional management: a set of guidelines', *Journal of Small Business Management*, 18(1), pp. 1–10.

Cho, J., Lee, K.-Y. and Lee, J. (2011) 'Dismissal law and human resource management in SMEs: lessons from Korea', *Asia Pacific Journal of Human Resources*, 49(1), pp. 105–123.

Churchill, N.C. and Lewis, V.L. (1983) 'The five stages of business growth', *Harvard Business Review*, May–June, pp. 30–50.

Cliff, J.E. (1998) 'Does one size fit all? Exploring the relationship between attitudes towards growth, gender, and business size', *Journal of Business Venturing*, 13, pp. 523–542.

Coad, A., Frankish, J., Roberts, R.G. and Storey, D.J. (2013) 'Growth paths and survival chances: an application of Gambler's Ruin theory', *Journal of Business Venturing*, 28(5), pp. 615–632.

Cox, A. (2005) 'Managing variable pay systems in smaller workplaces: the significance of employee perceptions of organisational justice.' In Marlow, S., Patton, D. and Ram, M. (eds) *Managing labour in small firms*. London: Routledge, pp. 97–109.

Curran, J. (2006) '"Specificity" and "denaturing" the small business', *International Small Business Journal*, 24(2), pp. 205–210.

Curran, J. and Stanworth, J. (1981) 'The social dynamics of the small manufacturing enterprise', *Journal of Management Studies*, 18(2), pp. 141–158.

Curran, J. and Stanworth, J. (1982) 'Bolton ten years on – a research inventory and critical review.' In Stanworth, J., Westrip, A. and Watkins, D. (eds) *Perspectives on a decade of small business research: Bolton ten years on*. Aldershot: Gower, pp. 3–28.

D'Angelo, A., Majocchi, A., Zucchella, A. and Buck, T. (2013) 'Geographical pathways for SME internationalization: insights from an Italian sample', *International Marketing Review*, 30(2), pp. 80–105.

Dannreuther, C. and Perren, L. (2013a) *The political economy of the small firm*. Abingdon: Routledge.

Dannreuther, C. and Perren, L. (2013b) 'Uncertain states: the political construction of the small firm, the individualisation of risk and the financial crisis', *Capital & Class*, 37(1), pp. 37–64.

Debrah, Y.A. and Mmieh, F. (2009) 'Employment relations in small- and medium-sized enterprises: insights from Ghana', *The International Journal of Human Resource Management*, 20(7), pp. 1554–1575.

Delerue, H. and Lejeune, A. (2010) 'Job mobility restriction mechanisms and appropriability in organizations: the mediating role of secrecy and lead time', *Technovation*, 30(5), pp. 359–366.

Delmotte, J., De Winne, S. and Sels, L. (2012) 'Toward an assessment of perceived HRM system strength: scale development and validation', *The International Journal of Human Resource Management*, 23(7), pp. 1481–1506.

Devins, D. and Johnson, S. (2003) 'Training and development activities in SMEs: some findings from an evaluation of the ESF Objective 4 programme in Britain', *International Small Business Journal*, 21(2), pp. 213–228.

Doherty, L. and Norton, A. (2014) 'Making and measuring "good" HR practice in an SME: the case of a Yorkshire bakery', *Employee Relations*, 36(2), pp. 128–147.

Drummond, I. and Stone, I. (2007) 'Exploring the potential of high performance work systems in SMEs', *Employee Relations*, 29(2), pp. 192–207.

DuGay, P. (1996) *Consumption and identity at work*. London: SAGE.

Dundon, T., Grugulis, I. and Wilkinson, A. (1999) 'Looking out of the black-hole', *Employee Relations*, 21(3), pp. 251–266.

Dyer, L. and Reeves, T. (1995) 'Human resource strategies and firm performance: what do we know and where do we need to go?', *The International Journal of Human Resource Management*, 6(3), pp. 656–670.

*The Economist* (2014) 'The binds that tie: a union walkout shows how hard reform will be for the government', 12 July. www.economist.com/news/europe/21606866-union-walkout-shows-how-hard-reform-will-be-government-binds-tie (accessed 23 December 2014).

Edwards, P.K. (1986) *Conflict at work: a materialist analysis of workplace relations*. Oxford: Basil Blackwell.

Edwards, P.K. (1995) 'From industrial relations to the employment relationship: the development of research in Britain', *Relations industrielles/Industrial Relations*, 50(1), pp. 39–65.

Edwards, P. and Ram, M. (2006) 'Surviving on the margins of the economy: working relationships in small, low-wage firms', *Journal of Management Studies*, 43(4), pp. 895–916.

Edwards, P. and Ram, M. (2010) 'HRM in small firms: respecting an regulating informality.' In Wilkinson, A., Bacon, N., Redman, T. and Snell, S. (eds) *The Sage handbook of human resource management*. London: SAGE, pp. 524–540.

Edwards, P., Ram, M. and Black, J. (2004) 'Why does employment legislation not damage small firms?', *Journal of Law and Society*, 31(2), pp. 245–265.

Edwards, P., Ram, M., Gupta, S.S. and Tsai, C.-J. (2006) 'The structuring of working relationships in small firms: towards a formal framework', *Organization*, 13(5), pp. 701–724.

Edwards, T. (2007) 'A critical account of knowledge management: agentic orientation and SME innovation', *International Journal of Entrepreneurial Behaviour & Research*, 13(2), pp. 64–81.

Edwards, T., Delbridge, R. and Munday, M. (2007) 'A critical assessment of the evaluation of EU interventions for innovation in the SME sector in Wales', *Urban Studies*, 44(12), pp. 2429–2447.

Fletcher, D. (2010) '"Life-making or risk taking"? Co-preneurship and family business start-ups', *International Small Business Journal*, 28(5), pp. 452–469.

Ford, J.D. and Schellenberg, D.A. (1982) 'Conceptual issues of linkage in the assessment of organizational performance', *The Academy of Management Review*, 7(1), pp. 49–58.

Forth, J., Bewley, H. and Bryson, A.R. (2006) *Small and medium-sized enterprises: findings from the 2004 Workplace Employment Relations Survey*. London: Department of Trade and Industry; Economic and Social Research Council; Advisory, Conciliation and Arbitration Service; Policy Studies Institute.

FSB (Federation of Small Businesses) (2015) *About the FSB*. www.fsb.org.uk/about (accessed 5 February 2015).

Fuller, T. (2003) 'If you wanted to know the future of small business what questions would you ask?', *Futures*, 35(4), pp. 305–321.

Gao, S.G., Sung, M.C. and Zhang, J. (2013) 'Risk management capability building in SMEs: a social capital perspective', *International Small Business Journal*, 31(6), pp. 677–700.

Gibb, A.A. (1997) 'Small firms' training and competitiveness: building upon the small business as a learning organisation', *International Small Business Journal*, 15(3), pp. 13–29.

Gibb, A.A. (2000) 'SME policy, academic research and the growth of ignorance, mythical concepts, myths, assumptions, rituals and confusions', *International Small Business Journal*, 18(3), pp. 13–35.

Gill, J. (1985) *Factors affecting the survival and growth of the smaller company*. Aldershot: Gower Publishing Co. Ltd.

Gilman, M.W. and Edwards, P.K. (2008) 'Testing a framework of the organization of small firms: fast-growth, high-tech SMEs', *International Small Business Journal*, 26(5), pp. 531–558.

Gilman, M., Edwards, P., Ram, M. and Arrowsmith, J. (2002) 'Pay determination in small firms in the UK: the case of the response to the National Minimum Wage', *Industrial Relations Journal*, 33(1), pp. 52–67.

Goffee, R. and Scase, R. (1995) *Corporate realities: dynamics of large and small organisations*. London: International Thomson Business Press.

Goss, D. (1991) *Small business and society*. London: Routledge.

Goss, D. and Jones, R. (1992) 'Organisation, structure and SME training provision', *International Small Business Journal*, 10(4), pp. 13–25.

Gray, C. (1998) *Enterprise and culture*. London: Routledge.

Greene, F.J., Mole, K.F. and Storey, D.J. (2008) *Three decades of enterprise culture: entrepreneurship, economic regeneration and public policy*. Basingstoke: Palgrave Macmillan.

Greer, C.R., Carr, J.C. and Hipp, L. (2015) 'Strategic staffing and small-firm performance', *Human Resource Management*, EarlyView Wiley Online Library. http://onlinelibrary.wiley.com/doi/10.1002/hrm.21693.pdf (accessed 15 March 2015).

Guest, D.E. (2011) 'Human resource management and performance: still searching for some answers', *Human Resource Management Journal*, 21(1), pp. 3–13.

Harney, B. and Dundon, T. (2006) 'Capturing complexity: developing an integrated approach to analysing HRM in SMEs', *Human Resource Management Journal*, 16(1), pp. 48–73.

Harney, B. and Dundon, T. (2007) 'An emergent theory of HRM: A theoretical and empirical exploration of determinants of HRM among Irish small- to medium-sized enterprises (SMEs)', *Advances in Industrial and Labor Relations*, 15, pp. 103–153.

Harris, L. (2000) 'Employment regulation and owner-managers in small firms: seeking support and guidance', *Journal of Small Business and Enterprise Development*, 7(4), pp. 352–362.

Hart, M. and Blackburn, R. (2005) 'Labour regulation and SMEs: A challenge to competitiveness and employability?' In Marlow, S., Patton, D. and Ram, M. (eds) *Managing labour in small firms*. London: Routledge, pp. 72–86.

Hendry, C., Jones, A. and Arthur, M. (1991). 'Skill supply, training and development in the small-medium enterprise', *International Small Business Journal*, 10(1), pp. 68–72.

Heneman, H.G., III and Berkley, R.A. (1999) 'Applicant attraction practices and outcomes among small businesses', *Journal of Small Business Management*, 37(1), pp. 53–74.

Hirschsohn, P. (2008) 'Regulating the "animal spirits" of entrepreneurs? Skills development in South African small and medium enterprises', *International Small Business Journal*, 26(2), pp. 181–206.

Holliday, R. (1995) *Investigating small firms: nice work?* London: Routledge.

Hoque, K. and Bacon, N. (2006) 'The antecedents of training activity in British small and medium-sized enterprises', *Work, Employment & Society*, 20(3), pp. 531–552.

Hoque, K. and Bacon, N. (2008) 'Investors in People and training in the British SME sector', *Human Relations*, 61(4), pp. 451–482.

Hoque, K. and Noon, M. (2004) 'Equal opportunities policy and practice in Britain: evaluating the "empty shell" hypothesis', *Work, Employment and Society*, 18(3), pp. 481–506.

Huang, T.-C. (2001) 'The relation of training practices and organizational performance in small and medium size enterprises', *Education & Training*, 43(8/9), pp. 437–444.

Huselid, M. (1995) 'The impact of human resource management practices on turnover, productivity, and corporate financial performance', *The Academy of Management Journal*, 38(3), pp. 635–672.

Ingham, G.K. (1970) *Size of industrial organization & worker behaviour*. London: Cambridge University Press.

Jameson, S.M. (2000) 'Recruitment and training in small firms', *Journal of European Industrial Training*, 24(1), pp. 43–49.

Jayasinghe, K., Thomas, D. and Wickramasinghe, D. (2008) 'Bounded emotionality in entrepreneurship: an alternative framework', *International Journal of Entrepreneurial Behaviour & Research*, 14(4), pp. 242–258.

Jayawarna, D., Macpherson, A. and Wilson, A. (2007) 'Training commitment and performance in manufacturing SMEs: incidence, intensity and approaches', *Journal of Small Business and Enterprise Development*, 14(2), pp. 321–338.

Jayawarna, D., Rouse, J. and Kitching, J. (2013) 'Entrepreneur motivations and life course', *International Small Business Journal*, 31(1), pp. 34–56.

Jennings, P. and Beaver, G. (1997) 'The performance and competitive advantage of small firms: a management perspective', *International Small Business Journal*, 15(2), pp. 63–75.

Jones, C. and Spicer, A. (2009) *Unmasking the entrepreneur*. Cheltenham: Edward Elgar Publishing Ltd.

Jones, J.T. (2005) 'The determinants of training in Australian manufacturing SMEs', *Education + Training*, 47(8/9), pp. 605–615.

Jones, P., Benyon, M.J., Pickernell, D. and Packham, G. (2013) 'Evaluating the impact of different training methods on SME business performance', *Environment and Planning C: Government and Policy*, 31(1), pp. 56–81.

Jordan, E., Thomas, A.P., Kitching, J.W. and Blackburn, R.A. (2013) *Employment regulation: Part A: employer perceptions and the impact of employment regulation*. London: Department for Business, Innovation and Skills.

## Bibliography

Kitching, J. (2006) 'Can small businesses help reduce employment exclusion?', *Environment and Planning C: Government and Policy*, 24(6), pp. 869–884.

Kitching, J. (2007) 'Regulating employment relations through workplace learning: a study of small employers', *Human Resource Management Journal*, 17(1), pp. 42–57.

Kitching, J. (2015) 'Between vulnerable compliance and confident ignorance: small employers, regulatory discovery practices and external support networks', *International Small Business Journal*, online. http://isb.sagepub.com/content/early/2015/02/13/0266242615569325.full.pdf+html (accessed 15 March 2015).

Kitching, J. and Blackburn, R. (1999) 'Management training and networking in small and medium-sized enterprises in three European regions: implications for business support', *Environment and Planning C: Government and Policy*, 17(5), pp. 621–635.

Kitching, J. and Blackburn, R. (2002) *The nature of training and motivation to train in small firms*. Research Report RR330. London: Department for Education and Skills.

Kitching, J., Hart, M. and Wilson, N. (2015) 'Burden or benefit? Regulation as a dynamic influence on small business performance', *International Small Business Journal*, 33(2), pp. 130–147.

Kitching, J., Kašperová, E. and Collis, J. (2013) The contradictory consequences of regulation: the influence of filing abbreviated accounts on UK small company performance, *International Small Business Journal*, online. http://isb.sagepub.com/content/early/2014/03/12/0266242613503973 (accessed 15 March 2015).

Kiviluoto, N. (2013) 'Growth as evidence of firm success: myth or reality?', *Entrepreneurship & Regional Development*, 25(7/8), pp. 569–586.

Klaas, B.S., McClendon, J.A. and Gainey, T.W. (2000) 'Managing HR in small and medium enterprises: the impact of professional employer organizations', *Entrepreneurship Theory & Practice*, 25(1), pp. 107–124.

Kondo, D.K. (1990) *Crafting selves: power, gender, and discourses of identity in a Japanese workplace*. Chicago, IL: The University of Chicago Press.

Kopina, H. (2005) 'Family matters? Recruitment methods and cultural boundaries in Singapore Chinese small and medium enterprises', *Asia Pacific Business Review*, 11(4), pp. 483–499.

Kotey, B. and Folker, C. (2007) 'Employee training in SMEs: effect of size and firm type – family and non-family', *Journal of Small Business Management*, 45(2), pp. 214–238.

Kotey, B. and Sheridan, A. (2004) 'Changing HRM practices with firm growth', *Journal of Small Business and Enterprise Development*, 11(4), pp. 474–485.

Kotey, B. and Slade, P. (2005) 'Formal human resource management practices in small growing firms', *Journal of Small Business Management*, 43(1), pp. 16–40.

Lange, T., Ottens, M. and Taylor, A. (2000) 'SMEs and barriers to skills development: a Scottish perspective', *Journal of European Industrial Training*, 24(1), pp. 5–11.

Leung, A., Zhang, J., Wong, P.K. and Foo, M.D. (2006) 'The use of networks in human resource acquisition for entrepreneurial firms: multiple "fit" considerations', *Journal of Business Venturing*, 21(5), pp. 664–686.

Levie, J. and Lichtenstein, B.B. (2010) 'A terminal assessment of stages theory: introducing a dynamic states approach to entrepreneurship', *Entrepreneurship Theory & Practice*, 34(2), pp. 317–350.

Lynch, L.M. (1994) *Training and the private sector: international comparisons*. Chicago, IL: National Bureau of Economic Research/The University of Chicago Press.

Lynch, L.M. and Black, S.E. (1998) 'Beyond the incidence of employer-provided training', *Industrial and Labor Relations Review*, 52(1), pp. 64–81.

MacDonald, S., Assimakopoulos, D. and Anderson, P. (2007) 'Education and training for innovation in SMEs: a tale of exploitation', *International Small Business Journal*, 25 (1), pp. 77–95.

Macmillan Committee (1931) *Report of the Committee on Finance and Industry*. London: His Majesty's Stationery Office.

Macpherson, A. and Jayawarna, D. (2007) 'Training approaches in manufacturing SMEs: measuring the influence of ownership, structure and markets', *Education + Training*, 49(8/9), pp. 698–719.

Mallett, O. and Wapshott, R. (2014) 'Informality and employment relationships in small firms: humour, ambiguity and straight-talking', *British Journal of Management*, 25(1), pp. 118–132.

Mallett, O. and Wapshott, R. (2015) 'Contesting the history and politics of enterprise and entrepreneurship', *Work, Employment & Society*, 29(1), pp. 177–182.

Mambula, C. (2002) 'Perceptions of SME growth constraints in Nigeria', *Journal of Small Business Management*, 40(1), pp. 58–65.

Marchington, M., Carroll, M. and Boxall, P. (2003) 'Labour scarcity and the survival of small firms: a resource-based view of the road haulage industry', *Human Resource Management Journal*, 13(4), pp. 5–22.

Marlow, S. (2003) 'Formality and informality in employment relations: the implications for regulatory compliance by smaller firms', *Environment and Planning C: Government and Policy*, 21(4), pp. 531–547.

Marlow, S. and Patton, D. (1993) 'Managing the employment relationship in the smaller firm: possibilities for human resource management', *International Small Business Journal*, 11(4), pp. 57–64.

Marlow, S., Taylor, S. and Thompson, A. (2010) 'Informality and formality in medium-sized companies: contestation and synchronization', *British Journal of Management*, 21(4), pp. 954–966.

Martin, A., Mactaggart, D. and Bowden, J. (2006) 'The barriers to the recruitment and retention of supervisors/managers in the Scottish tourism industry', *International Journal of Contemporary Hospitality Management*, 18(5), pp. 380–397.

Martin, L.M., Janjuha-Jivraj, S., Carey, C. and Reddy, S.S. (2004) 'Formalizing relationships? Time, change and the psychological contract in team entrepreneurial companies.' In Barrett, R. and Mayson, S. (eds) *International handbook of entrepreneurship and HRM*. Cheltenham: Edward Elgar, pp. 205–223.

Massey, C. (2004) 'Employee practices in New Zealand SMEs', *Employee Relations*, 26(1), pp. 94–105.

Matlay, H. (1997) 'The paradox of training in the small business sector of the British economy', *Journal of Vocational Education and Training*, 49(4), pp. 573–589.

Matlay, H. (2002) 'Industrial relations in the SME sector of the British economy: an empirical perspective', *Journal of Small Business and Enterprise Development*, 9(3), pp. 307–318.

Messersmith, J.G. and Wales, W.J. (2013) 'Entrepreneurial orientation and performance in young firms: the role of human resource management', *International Small Business Journal*, 31(2), pp. 115–136.

Miller, D. (1992) 'The Icarus Paradox: how exceptional companies bring about their own downfall', *Business Horizons*, January/February, pp. 24–35.

Mills, C.W. (1951) *White collar: the American middle class*. Oxford: Oxford University Press.

Mintzberg, H. (1980) 'Structure in 5s: a synthesis of the research on organization design', *Management Science*, 26(3), pp. 322–341.

Misztal, B.A. (2000) *Informality: social theory and contemporary practice*. London: Routledge.

Mohr, A. and Shoobridge, G. (2011) 'The role of multi-ethnic workforces in the internationalisation of SMEs', *Journal of Small Business and Enterprise Development*, 18(4), pp. 748–763.

Morris, D., Collier, T. and Wood, G. (2005) 'Effects of minimum wage legislation: some evidence from small enterprises in the UK', *International Small Business Journal*, 23(2), pp. 191–209.

Moule, C. (1998) 'Regulation of work in small firms: a view from the inside', *Work, Employment & Society*, 12(4), pp. 635–653.

Mueller, F. (1996) 'Human resources as strategic assets: an evolutionary resource-based theory', *Journal of Management Studies*, 33(6), pp. 757–785.

Nadin, S. and Cassell, C. (2007) 'New deal for old? Exploring the psychological contract in a small firm environment', *International Small Business Journal*, 25(4), pp. 417–443.

Nooteboom, B. (1988) 'The facts about small business and the real values of its "life world": a social philosophical interpretation of this sector of the modern economy', *American Journal of Economics and Sociology*, 47(3), pp. 299–314.

Paauwe, J. and Boselie, P. (2005) 'HRM and performance: what next?', *Human Resource Management Journal*, 15(4), pp. 68–83.

Packham, G., Miller, C.J., Thomas, B.C. and Brooksbank, D. (2005) 'An examination of the management challenges faced by growing SCEs in South Wales', *Construction Innovation*, 5(1), pp. 13–25.

Pajo, K., Coetzer, A. and Guenole, N. (2010) 'Formal development opportunities and withdrawal behaviors by employees in small and medium-sized enterprises', *Journal of Small Business Management*, 48(3), pp. 281–301.

Park, S., Kim, B.-Y., Jang, W. and Nam, K.-M. (2014) 'Imperfect information and labor market bias against small and medium-sized enterprises: a Korean case', *Small Business Economics*, online. http://download.springer.com/static/pdf/214/art%253A10.1007%252Fs11187-014-9571-7.pdf?auth66=1426438613_3fce7e1ca2b665b196ec3358e4c478a1&ext=.pdf (accessed 15 March 2015).

Patel, P.C. and Conklin, B. (2012) 'Perceived labor productivity in small firms – the effects of high-performance work systems and group culture through employee retention', *Entrepreneurship Theory & Practice*, 36(2), pp. 205–235.

Patton, D., Marlow, S. and Hannon, P. (2000) 'The relationship between training and small firm performance: research frameworks and lost quests', *International Small Business Journal*, 19(1), pp. 11–27.

Patzelt, H., Knyphausen-Aufsess, D. and Nikol, P. (2008) 'Top management teams, business models, and performance of biotechnology ventures: an upper echelon perspective', *British Journal of Management*, 19(3), pp. 205–221.

Penrose, E.T. (1959) *The theory of the growth of the firm*. Oxford: Basil Blackwell.

Perraudin, C., Thèvenot, N. and Valentin, J. (2013) 'Avoiding the employment relationship: outsourcing and labour substitution among French manufacturing firms, 1984–2003', *International Labour Review*, 152(3–4), pp. 525–547.

Perrow, C. (1970) *Organizational analysis: a sociological view*. London: Tavistock Publications.

Phelps, R., Adams, R. and Bessant, J. (2007) 'Life cycles of growing organizations: a review with implications for knowledge and learning', *International Journal of Management Reviews*, 9(1), pp. 1–30.

Purcell, J. (1999) 'Best practice and best fit: chimera or cul-de-sac?', *Human Resource Management Journal*, 9(3), pp. 26–41.

Rainnie, A. (1985) 'Small firms, big problems: the political economy of small businesses', *Capital & Class*, 9, pp. 140–168.

Rainnie, A. (1989) *Industrial relations in small firms: small isn't beautiful.* London: Routledge.

Rainnie, A. (1991) 'Small firms: between the enterprise culture and new times.' In Burrows, R. (ed.) *Deciphering the enterprise culture: entrepreneurship, petty capitalism and the restructuring of Britain.* London: Routledge, pp. 176–199.

Ram, M. (1991) 'The dynamics of workplace relations in small firms', *International Small Business Journal*, 10(1), pp. 44–53.

Ram, M. (1994) *Managing to survive: working lives in small firms.* Oxford: Blackwell.

Ram, M. (1999) 'Managing autonomy: employment relations in small professional service firms', *International Small Business Journal*, 17(2), pp. 13–30.

Ram, M. (2000) 'Investors in People in small firms: case study evidence from the business services sector', *Personnel Review*, 29(1), pp. 69–91.

Ram, M. and Edwards, P. (2003) 'Praising Caesar not burying him: what we know about employment relations in small firms', *Work, Employment & Society*, 17(4), pp. 719–730.

Ram, M. and Edwards, P. (2010) 'Industrial relations in small firms.' In Colling, T. and Terry, M. (eds) *Industrial relations: theory and practice.* Chichester: Wiley, pp. 231–252.

Ram, M., Edwards, P., Gilman, M. and Arrowsmith, J. (2001) 'The dynamics of informality: employment relations in small firms and effects of regulatory change', *Work, Employment & Society*, 15(4), pp. 845–861.

Ramsay, H., Scholarios, D. and Harley, B. (2000) 'Employees and high-performance work systems: testing inside the black box', *British Journal of Industrial Relations*, 38(4), pp. 501–531.

Reich, W. (2010) 'Three problems of intersubjectivity – and one solution', *Sociological Theory*, 28(1), pp. 40–63.

Revans, R.W. (1956) 'Industrial morale and size of unit', *The Political Quarterly*, 27(3), pp. 303–311.

Rousseau, D.M., Sitkin, S.B., Burt, R.S. and Camerer, C. (1998) 'Not so different after all: a cross-discipline view of trust', *Academy of Management Review*, 23(3), pp. 393–404.

Rubery, J. (1994) 'Internal and external labour markets: towards an integrated analysis.' In Rubery, J. and Wilkinson, F. (eds) *Employer strategy and the labour market.* Oxford: Oxford University Press, pp. 37–68.

Saridakis, G., Muñoz Torres, R. and Johnstone, S. (2013) 'Do human resource practices enhance organizational commitment in SMEs with low employee satisfaction?', *British Journal of Management*, 24(3), pp. 445–458.

Saridakis, G., Sen-Gupta, S., Edwards, P. and Storey, D.J. (2008) 'The impact of enterprise size on employment tribunal incidence and outcomes: evidence from Britain', *British Journal of Industrial Relations*, 46(3), pp. 469–499.

Scase, R. (1995) 'Employment relations in small firms.' In Edwards, P. (ed.) *Industrial relations: theory and practice in Britain.* Oxford: Blackwell, pp. 569–595.

Scase, R. and Goffee, R. (1982) *The entrepreneurial middle class.* London: Croom Helm.

Scase, R. and Goffee, R. (1987) *The real world of the small business owner* (2nd edn). London: Croom Helm.

Schlosser, F. (2014) 'Differences in key employees by firm age and entrepreneurial orientation.' In Blackburn, R., Delmar, F., Fayolle, A. and Welter, F. (eds) *Entrepreneurship, people and organisations: frontiers in European entrepreneurship research.* Cheltenham: Edward Elgar Publishing, pp. 74–93.

Schlosser, F. (2015) 'Identifying and differentiating key employees from owners and other employees in SMEs', *Journal of Small Business Management*, 53(1), pp. 37–53.

Schumacher, E.F. (1973) *Small is beautiful: a study of economics as if people mattered*. London: Blond & Briggs Ltd.

Scott, M. and Rainnie, A. (1982) 'Beyond Bolton: industrial relations in the small firm.' In Stanworth, J., Westrip, A., Watkins, D. and Lewis, J. (eds) *Perspectives on a decade of small business research: Bolton 10 years on*. Aldershot: Gower, pp. 159–178.

Scott, M., Roberts, I., Holroyd, G. and Sawbridge, D. (1989) *Management and industrial relations in small firms*, Research Paper 70. London: Department of Employment.

Sels, L., De Winne, S., Maes, J., Delmotte, J., Faems, D. and Forrier, A. (2006a) 'Unravelling the HRM–performance link: value-creating and cost-increasing effects of small business HRM', *Journal of Management Studies*, 43(2), pp. 319–342.

Sels, L., De Winne, S., Delmotte, J., Maes, J., Faems, D. and Forrier, A. (2006b) 'Linking HRM and small business performance: an examination of the impact of HRM intensity on the productivity and financial performance of small businesses', *Small Business Economics*, 26(1), pp. 83–101.

Sharifi, S. and Zhang, M. (2009) 'Sense-making and recipes: examples from selected small firms', *International Journal of Entrepreneurial Behaviour & Research*, 15(6), pp. 555–570.

Shaw, J.D., Delery, J.E., Jenkins, J.G.D. and Gupta, N. (1998) 'An organization-level analysis of voluntary and involuntary turnover', *Academy of Management Journal*, 41(5), pp. 511–525.

Sheehan, M. (2014) 'Human resource management and performance: evidence from small and medium-sized firms', *International Small Business Journal*, 32(5), pp. 545–570.

Shutt, J. and Whittington, R. (1987) 'Fragmentation strategies and the rise of small units: cases from the North West', *Regional Studies*, 21(1), pp. 13–23.

Sisson, K. (1993) 'In search of HRM', *British Journal of Industrial Relations*, 31(2), pp. 201–210.

Sloan, B. and Chittenden, F. (2006) 'Fiscal policy and self-employment: targeting business growth', *Environment and Planning C: Government and Policy*, 24(1), pp. 83–98.

Smallbone, D., Supri, S. and Baldock, R. (2000) 'The implications of new technology for the skill and training needs of small and medium-sized printing firms', *Education + Training*, 42(4/5), pp. 299–307.

Smith, A.J., Boocock, J.L.-C. and Whittaker, J. (2002) 'IiP and SMEs: awareness, benefits and barriers', *Personnel Review*, 31(1), pp. 62–85.

Smith, C. (2006) 'The double indeterminacy of labour power: labour effort and labour mobility', *Work, Employment & Society*, 20(2), pp. 389–402.

Stinchcombe, A.L. (1965) 'Social structure and organizations.' In March, J.G. (ed.) *Handbook of organizations*. Chicago, IL: Rand McNally College Publishing Co.

Stinchcombe, A.L. (2001) *When formality works: authority and abstraction in law and organizations*. Chicago, IL and London: The University of Chicago Press.

Storey, D.J. (1994) *Understanding the small business sector*. London: Routledge.

Storey, D.J. (2002) 'Education, training and development policies and practices in medium-sized companies in the UK: do they really influence firm performance?', *Omega*, 30(4), pp. 249–264.

Storey, D.J. (2004) 'Exploring the link, among small firms, between management training and firm performance: a comparison between the UK and other OECD countries', *The International Journal of Human Resource Management*, 15(1), pp. 112–130.

Storey, D.J. (2011) 'Optimism and chance: the elephants in the entrepreneurship room', *International Small Business Journal*, 29(4), pp. 303–321.

Storey, D.J. and Westhead, P. (1997) 'Management training in small firms – a case of market failure?', *Human Resource Management Journal*, 7(2), pp. 61–71.

Swart, J. and Kinnie, N. (2003) 'Knowledge-intensive firms: the influence of the client on HR systems', *Human Resource Management Journal*, 13(3), pp. 37–55.

Tanova, C. and Nadiri, H. (2005) 'Recruitment and training policies and practices: the case of Turkey as an EU candidate', *Journal of European Industrial Training*, 29(9), pp. 694–711.

Taylor, S. (2005) 'The hunting of the Snark: a critical analysis of human resource management discourses in relation to managing labour in smaller organisations.' In Marlow, S., Patton, D. and Ram, M. (eds) *Managing labour in small firms*. Abingdon: Routledge, pp. 18–42.

Taylor, S., Thorpe, R. and Down, S. (2002) 'Negotiating managerial legitimacy in smaller organizations: management education, technical skill and situated competence', *Journal of Management Education*, 26(5), pp. 550–573.

Timming, A.R. (2011) 'What do tattoo artists know about HRM? Recruitment and selection in the body art sector', *Employee Relations*, 33(5), pp. 570–584.

Tocher, N. and Rutherford, M.W. (2009) 'Perceived acute human resource management problems in small and medium firms: an empirical examination', *Entrepreneurship Theory & Practice*, 33(2), pp. 455–479.

Torrès, O. (2003) 'Thirty years of research into SMEs: tends and counter-trends in the quest for disciplinarity.' In Watkins, D. (ed.) *Annual review of progress in entrepreneurship research, volume 2, 2002–2003*. Brussels: European Foundation for Management Development, pp. 37–84.

Torrès, O. and Julien, P.-A. (2005) 'Specificity and denaturing of small business', *International Small Business Journal*, 23(4), pp. 355–377.

Tsai, C., Sengupta, S. and Edwards, P. (2007) 'When and why is small beautiful? The experience of work in the small firm', *Human Relations*, 60(12), pp. 1779–1807.

Urwin, P. and Buscha, F. (2012) *Back to work: the role of small businesses in employment and enterprise*. London: Federation of Small Businesses.

Verreynne, M.-L., Parker, P. and Wilson, M. (2013) 'Employment systems in small firms: a multilevel analysis', *International Small Business Journal*, 31(4), pp. 405–431.

Vickerstaff, S. (1992) 'The training needs of small firms', *Human Resource Management Journal*, 2(3), pp. 1–15.

Wapshott, R. and Mallett, O. (2012) 'The spatial implications of homeworking: a Lefebvrian approach to the rewards and challenges of home-based work', *Organization*, 19(1), pp. 63–79.

Wapshott, R. and Mallett, O. (2013) 'The unspoken side of mutual adjustment: understanding intersubjective negotiation in small professional service firms', *International Small Business Journal*, 31(8), pp. 978–996.

Wapshott, R., Mallett, O. and Spicer, D. (2014) 'Exploring change in small firms' HRM practices.' In Machado, C.F. and Davim, J.P. (eds) *Work organization and human resource management*. London: Springer, pp. 73–92.

Watson, T.J. (1995) 'Entrepreneurship and professional management: a fatal distinction', *International Small Business Journal*, 13(2), pp. 34–46.

Way, S.A. (2002) 'High performance work systems and intermediate indicators of firm performance within the US small business sector', *Journal of Management*, 28(6), pp. 765–785.

Weatherill, B. and Cope, J. (1969) *Acorns to oaks: a policy for small business*. London: Conservative Political Centre, No. 426.

# Bibliography

Welsh, J.A. and White, J.F. (1981) 'A small business is not a little big business', *Harvard Business Review*, July–August, pp. 18–32.

Westhead, P. (1998) 'Factors associated with the provision of job-related formal training by employers', *International Journal of Entrepreneurial Behaviour & Research*, 4(3), pp. 187–216.

Westrip, A. (1986) 'Small firms policy: the case of employment legislation.' In Curran, J., Stanworth, J. and Watkins, D. (eds) *The survival of the small firm, volume 2: employment, growth, technology and politics.* Aldershot: Gower Publishing Co. Ltd, pp. 184–203.

Wiesner, R. and Innes, P. (2010) 'Bleak house or bright prospect? HRM in Australian SMEs over 1998–2008', *Asia Pacific Journal of Human Resources*, 48(2), pp. 151–184.

Wilkinson, A. (1999) 'Employment relations in SMEs', *Employee Relations*, 21(3), pp. 206–217.

Williams, C.C. (2007) *Rethinking the future of work: directions and visions.* Basingstoke: Palgrave Macmillan.

Williamson, I.O. (2000) 'Employer legitimacy and recruitment success in small businesses', *Entrepreneurship Theory & Practice*, 25(1), pp. 27–42.

Wright, P.M. and Boswell, W.R. (2002) 'Desegregating HRM: a review and synthesis of micro and macro human resource management research', *Journal of Management*, 28(3), pp. 247–276.

Wright, P.M., McMahan, G.C. and McWilliams, A. (1994) 'Human resources and sustained competitive advantage: a resource-based perspective', *The International Journal of Human Resource Management*, 5(2), pp. 301–326.

Young, D. (1992) 'Enterprise regained.' In Heelas, P. and Morris, P. (eds) *The values of the enterprise culture: the moral debate.* London: Routledge, pp. 29–35.

Young, D. (2012) 'Make business your business: supporting the start-up and development of small business', *URN* 12/827, May. www.gov.uk/government/uploads/system/uploads/attachment_data/file/32245/12-827-make-business-your-business-report-on-start-ups.pdf (accessed 11 August 2014).

Young, D. (2013) 'Growing your business: a report on growing micro businesses', *URN* 13/729, May. www.gov.uk/government/uploads/system/uploads/attachment_data/file/198165/growing-your-business-lord-young.pdf (accessed 11 August 2014).

Yu, F.-L. (2009) 'Towards a structural model of a small family business in Taiwan', *Journal of Small Business and Entrepreneurship*, 22(4), pp. 413–428.

Zheng, C., Morrison, M. and O'Neill, G. (2006) 'An empirical study of high performance HRM practices in Chinese SMEs', *The International Journal of Human Resource Management*, 17(10), pp. 1772–1803.

# Index

Ad hoc decision making 12–13, 40, 72–3, 81, 111–112, 115, 118–119
Advisory, Conciliation and Arbitration Service (Acas) 102–3
Arrowsmith, J. 41, 87–8, 92–3
Atkinson, C. 83, 87–8, 103–4, 106
Australia 80

Bacon, N. 75–6
Behrends, T. 54–6
Bennett, R. 10, 146
Blackburn, R. 64, 69–70, 79
Bleak house 35–6
Bolton Report 32–5, 78–9

Cameron, D. 113
Canada 24
Centre for Regional Economic and Enterprise Development 6
Change, organisational 27–9
China 80, 97
Clients 24, 51, 117
Coad, A. 116, 135
Compliance, regulatory 104
Confederation of British Industry 32–3
Cox, A. 87
Curran, J. 11, 33–5, 79–80
Cycling 71

Dannreuther, C. 31–5
Deficit model 54–6, 63, 80, 133–5, 139–140
Delegation 22–4
Denmark 69–70
Department for Business, Innovation & Skills 102
Department for Education and Skills 64
Dundon, T. 12, 55, 141

Edwards, P. 9, 18, 103–6, 136
Edwards, P., Gilman and Edwards framework 43–5, 84–5, 87, 141
Employee influence 89–93
Employment costs 21–2
Employment relationship, definition of 8–9
Employment relationships, interaction perspective of 40–3
Employment Tribunal 102–4
Empty shell 103, 116–117
Engineering 68
Entrepreneur, definition of 6–7
Entrepreneurship, definition of 6–7
Equivalence model 56–7
Estonia 4
Ethnography 40, 145
European Union (EU) 66
External influences 37–9, 51–2, 68, 84–86, 144

Federation of Small Businesses 19–20
Formal policies 101–2
Formalisation 112–120
France 60

Germany 69–70
Ghana 54, 82, 85–6
Gilman, M. see Edwards, P., Gilman and Edwards framework
Gray, C. 27
Growth 112–119
Growth, life-cycle models of 114–115
Growth, myth of 116
Growth, stages of 113

Harney, B. 12, 55, 141
High Performance Work Systems 100, 124–131

## 162   Index

High Performance Work Systems, employee experiences of 131–2
Holliday, R. 18, 40, 52
HRM (Human Resource Management), definition of 8, 55–6, 134–5 *see also* High Performance Work Systems

Icarus Paradox 28–9
Informal routinisation 133
Informality 12–13, 40, 50, 53–4, 72–6, 81–2, 101–2, 111–2
Informality, limitations of 57–60
Informality and formality, co-existance of 118–123, 142
Ingham, G.K. 78–80
Institute for Small Business and Entrepreneurship (ISBE) 6
International Monetary Fund (IMF) 101
International Small Business Journal 10, 127–8
Intersubjectivity 91–2
Investors in People 68, 103, 117, 130
Italy 38

Japan 38, 62
Job satisfaction 78–80
Julien, P.A. 10–12
Justice, perceptions of 87–9

Kitching, J. 52, 59, 64, 69–70, 106
Korea 62
Kotey, B. 58

Labour market 43–4, 67, 85–6, 91, 98–9
Legislation see Regulation
Lifestyle business 26–7, 61

Mallett, O. 6, 40–1, 90–1
Management speak 73–4
Management-style see Owner-manager prerogative
Manufacturing 33, 38, 42–3, 68, 99–100
Marlow, S. 12, 18, 89, 111, 119, 121
Mintzberg, H. 41
Misztal, B. 111
Motivations, employee 33–5
Moule, C. 39–40, 99
Mutual adjustment 41–3, 90–2, 143

National minimum wage 84–5, 92–3, 105
Negotiation 89–92, 99–100, 106
Networks 44, 58
New Labour 35, 139
Nigeria 71–2

Nursing homes 61–2

Office for National Statistics 5
Owner-manager 7, 21–9
Owner-manager, prerogative of 36, 44, 69–70, 83–4, 104, 113–114

Penrose, E. 125
Performance related pay 80–2, 117–118
Perren, L. 31–5
Phelps, R. 115
Policy, SME 65–6, 146
Politicisation of SMEs 138–9
Product market 44, 85
Professional services 10, 24, 57, 65, 82, 86, 88, 100
Proximity 13, 53, 83, 111, 114
Psychological contract 87–91
Purcell, J. 129

Rainnie, A. 12, 18, 36–40, 79–80, 85, 129
Ram, M. 18, 40–3, 53–4, 74, 111, 121
Recruitment 21–2
Recruitment practices 50–4
Recruitment, alternatives to 61–2
Red tape 104, 113
Redundancy criteria 117
Regulation 14, 59–60, 84–5, 92–3, 101–7, 113, 116
Regulations, impact of 104–6
Resource based view of the firm (RBV) 125
Resource poverty see Resources
Resources 13–14, 21, 44, 49–50, 64
Restaurants 42
Retail 54
Routines 14, 44, 81, 112
Rules and routines 44

Saridakis, G. 103
Scotland 51–2, 96
Sels, L. 126–7, 136
Sheehan, M. 100, 127–8, 130, 132–6
Singapore 62
Sisson, K. 36, 75
Skills 24–5, 58–9
Slade, A. 58
Small business specificity 10–11
Small firms, relation to large firms 38–9
Small is beautiful 32–5
SME, definition of 7–8, 12, 31–2
SMEs and politics 31–2
SMEs, employment and 4–5, 19

SMEs, growth of 19–20, 26–7
Social proximity see Proximity
Solicitors 61
Solicitors Regulation Authority 10
South Africa 59–60, 66–7
South Korea 101
Spatial proximity see Proximity
Staff retention 98–101
Staff turnover, involuntary 101–6
Staff turnover, voluntary 95–8
Stanworth, J. 33–5, 79–80
Stinchcombe, A.L. 14, 121
Storey, D. 77, 112
Strategic choice 44, 67

Tattoo studio 57
Taylor, S. 8
Thatcher, M. 35
Tipping points 29
Torrès, O. 10–12
Trade unions 33
Training and performance 66
Training, constraints on 69–72

Training, formal 63–4
Training, influences on 67
Training, investments in 70–1, 97
Training, on the job 73–5
Turkey 50

UK 4–5, 19–20, 38, 69–70, 80, 113
University of Sheffield 6
USA 4

Wales 23
Wapshott, R. 5–6, 40–1, 90–1
Watson, T. 29
Way, S.A. 124–6, 136
Working Families Tax Credits 105
Workplace Employment Relations Survey 36, 79, 103, 132
Workplace Industrial Relations Survey see Workplace Employment Relations Survey

Verreynne, M.-L. 131–3